I0142537

I Don't Know How to Be Okay

A Guide to Navigate the Journey of Grief and Loss

Missy Richardson, RN

Southern Roads Publishing

© **Copyright 2022 - All rights reserved.**

The content contained within this book may not be reproduced, duplicated or transmitted without direct written permission from the author or the publisher.

Under no circumstances will any blame or legal responsibility be held against the publisher, or author, for any damages, reparation, or monetary loss due to the information contained within this book, either directly or indirectly.

Legal Notice:

This book is copyright protected. It is only for personal use. You cannot amend, distribute, sell, use, quote or paraphrase any part, or the content within this book, without the consent of the author or publisher.

Disclaimer Notice:

Please note the information contained within this document is for educational and entertainment purposes only. All effort has been executed to present accurate, up to date, reliable, complete information. No warranties of any kind are declared or implied. Readers acknowledge that the author is not engaged in the rendering of legal, financial, medical or professional advice. The content within this book has been derived from various sources. Please consult a licensed professional before attempting any techniques outlined in this book.

By reading this document, the reader agrees that under no circumstances is the author responsible for any losses, direct or indirect, that are incurred as a result of the use of the information contained within this document, including, but not limited to, errors, omissions, or inaccuracies.

Table of Contents

Dedication

I dedicate this book to two
important people in my life,
Amber and Elizabeth.
Amber was my first teacher,
she taught me how to play, to
laugh, and showed me that it was
important to be who I truly am. She
also taught me about loss and grief.

Elizabeth taught me how to find
my voice, how to accept love, and
how to give it. She also taught
me to not give up on my dreams
and encouraged me to stay on
track and write this book.

This book is for everyone who has
lost someone they truly loved, I
hope it can help you to navigate
through and be able to know you
did make a difference in
their lives by loving them.
Grief is a difficult journey
and it's not for the
faint of heart!

Introduction

As a nurse, I witness death daily, but it doesn't hit home until someone I know has passed away. I lost my father years ago to cancer but, luckily, had my mother around a lot longer. 2012 was a tough year for me. I lost my best friend to breast cancer in January, my partner in March, and my mom in November. It seems I couldn't grieve one without losing another, but it was the loss of my partner that shook me to my core. The loss of my partner is when it hit me that I didn't know how to grieve, how to get through the sorrow and depression. I didn't know how to navigate that kind of loss. I would go from crying uncontrollably one minute to a panic attack the next. The thought of life continuing without her was not something I knew how to do. It has been 10 years and I can finally look back and thank God for the time that we did have together. That encounter taught me not only about love and grief, but also about life.

From the day we are born, we build relationships of all kinds, and we have new experiences along the way. People will remain with us for a lifetime, a short while, and others for even less time than that. Why is it that death strikes each of us so differently? Is it the permanence of their passing that makes it so hard? Does their death call to question your mortality? Unresolved feelings toward your loved one, or words left unsaid, make it so much harder to grieve properly. Understand that there is no time limit for you to decide you're ready to move on, nor is there any "right" way to grieve a loss. Chances are, even when you feel you've moved on, waves of emotion will come upon you at any time. It could be the way someone looks at you, a favorite song, or words that strike a chord and remind you explicitly of that person. Be prepared to react to ordinary things that remind you of your deceased loved one, because the simplest item can evoke a landslide of memories and emotions. This is normal!

I Don't Know How to Be Okay will help you to navigate through the loss of a loved one, assist you in making the necessary arrangements according to the wishes of the deceased, and how to get through the funeral, or celebration of life, and the lonely days that follow. Together, we will examine beliefs, myths, known truths, and the questions human beings have about the afterlife. More importantly, you will learn management tactics to subdue panic attacks, but also how to fully ride the rollercoaster of emotions that follow death and loss. You will learn to recognize in yourself the readiness to move on, find love after the loss of a spouse, and the importance of deliberate choices to avoid costly, impetuous decisions made at a time when you're at your most vulnerable. Hang on to the memories, enjoy reminiscing and reveling in the pleasant memories, accept the distressing and upsetting thoughts and allow them to pass through, and safeguard your mental health and emotional well-being. I will also tackle journal prompts to help you find an outlet for all these confusing emotions, and discuss the merits of exercise, your quiet place, and meditation to guide you through your days. Don't give up if it seems too hard at first; grief is a journey. With practice, you will objectively identify your feelings and triggers.

This book will help you find peace amid the chaos and control in a period of turmoil; it'll offer a way forward and help you recover a sense of love and trust. You're changed, but not destroyed. You will get through this challenging time and emerge stronger for it. Remember to pause and breathe, get up and stretch, or take a short walk if the emotions become too overwhelming. Take the time you need to let yourself fall apart so you can make room for better things to come.

In Memory Of
Amber Freeman
July 1974–March 2012

"GRIEF NEVER ENDS, BUT IT
CHANGES.
IT IS A PASSAGE, NOT A PLACE TO
STAY.
GRIEF IS NOT A SIGN OF WEAKNESS,
NOR A LACK OF FAITH.
IT IS THE PRICE OF LOVE."
-RUMI

Chapter 1

You Are Changed
but Not
Destroyed.

Your world can feel like it's splintering into a million different directions when someone you love dies. Whether it's a parent, spouse, lover, child, or close friend, it stirs up a whole maelstrom of emotions. Reality feels completely distorted. Perhaps stunned is a better description of this moment of absolute disruption.

I was discussing grief with my dear friend Elizabeth, and she told me her story. "I think the intention to thoroughly prepare for the end of your life so that you spare the ones you love the pain of having to manage after you're gone is always there," she said. "My mother was no exception. She paid for years on a funeral policy insurance that would cover her expenses when she passed. Unfortunately, her Social Security was not enough to sustain her everyday needs, and she had to cash out her funeral policy to pay the bills."

When Elizabeth's mother, Kathleen, was diagnosed with colon cancer and the doctor told them to prepare for her passing in approximately six months, I don't think either of them accepted that it was a reality at that point. Kathleen just wanted to do whatever she could while she could still walk, and while she was not yet debilitated by pain. She wasn't concerned with sorting her things or getting her paperwork in order; she just wanted to hold on to what little life she had left, so that's what she did. Together, they watched all of Kathleen's old favorite black and white movies, went to the casino to play the slot machines, and ate her favorite foods when she felt like eating.

Kathleen felt it was essential to read from the Bible every night, intending to read the entire thing to completion before she left this world. Elizabeth remembered one night her mother just stopped and closed the Bible, and she said, "I think I've been living a lie all my life believing in this book." Shortly after, she was in so much pain that she said it was time to go to the hospital.

Kathleen closed the lid on the piano keyboard, patted this beloved instrument goodbye, took a tour throughout the house, and she hugged the walls. She said her goodbyes to the sanctuary she called home. Elizabeth watched her in silence as she packed a small bag for the hospital, and somehow, they both knew that she would not return home again.

Kathleen was in and out of a morphine-induced haze, and when she was cognitive, she apologized for not having the funeral insurance available for Elizabeth to cremate her, which was her final wish. As Kathleen lay in her hospital bed, Elizabeth set up a GoFundMe page on her Facebook account to try to raise the fees to cover her mother's cremation. It was expected to cost around $1,400, a sum that they did not have available at the time. Elizabeth had taken time off from work and eventually needed to quit to be with her mother for the last six months of her life. Sadly, Kathleen passed in only five months. Elizabeth honestly felt cheated by losing the last month of the expected length of time with her. Within about six hours of posting the Go Fund Me, Elizabeth's friends had pitched in, and the entirety of the required funds had been raised to handle the cremation expenses. Elizabeth felt profoundly grateful. A week later, Kathleen crossed over to the beautiful realm of light and love.

In that hospital room, she squeezed Kathleen's hand and said, "Mom, you don't have to worry. My friends have all pitched in, and your cremation fees are paid." It seemed so morbid to tell her that while she lay there struggling to breathe, yet Elizabeth knew that somehow it would bring her mother peace of mind to see that burden lifted before she passed on.

In this section, you will learn how to cope with the death of a loved one and how to accept your new reality and experiences. Here, you will learn how to process your loss, accept that loss, and learn to understand that life has irrevocably changed, never to revert to what it was before. You will see that you're not alone and that nobody experiences grief the same as anyone else. You can silence the often-unhelpful advice from others to "move on," "get over it," and "let go." They mean well, but such words only serve to isolate you further at such a vulnerable time.

AM I IN A BAD DREAM?

It took Elizabeth two weeks to pick up her mother's ashes; Elizabeth just didn't dare to go to the Funeral Home to retrieve them. When she arrived at the Funeral Home, they handed her a black box inside a gift bag, of all things. It seemed surreal that seventy-five years of life would culminate in a box of ashes. Elizabeth felt very alone with no one to lean on, and she learned that no one wants to be around when you're grieving. She understood that; it's awkward for everyone involved. Elizabeth strapped Kathleen's ashes into the passenger seat, securing the seat belt around the package. Elizabeth looked down at the box and smiled. "I always wanted to strap your ash in, and now I've done that." It was an inside joke shared between them. It took Elizabeth another two weeks before she could carry her mother's ashes into the house that she called home.

Elizabeth was interning as a Rehabilitation Counselor at the time, staying in her mother's house. She sifted through all of Kathleen's things, shredded personal papers, and donated everything. She couldn't bear to see her mother's things because they would trigger uncontrollable sobbing. Kathleen would have felt awful for not dealing with those worldly possessions before she died. Elizabeth knew her mother didn't want her to have to manage so much, and it was one of the things she expressed that she was sorry for before she left.

I would say that grief does not come in any particular textbook stages because you go through it in whatever stages necessary to facilitate progress through the grieving process. Elizabeth stated that before her mother passed, Kathleen spoke to her son on the phone because he asked for her words of wisdom. "Have no regrets," she said, "because I have many." Elizabeth understood the impact of what she had said on a different level because of the life she led. Kathleen had such an unhappy childhood, never feeling like she was loved, and she never felt deserving of genuine love or acceptance. As a result, she built walls around her emotions all through her life to circumvent that missing piece, and she wound up pushing everyone away. Kathleen left the impression that she was both unhappy and a tyrant. Elizabeth, however, saw a five-year-old little girl who just wanted to be loved for who she was without society's conditions imposed upon her.

19

While you try to grapple with your loss, I'm sure your head is spinning with questions and frightening sensations. One could say coping with the passing of those you love is a bit like throwing a giant bucket of water into the air while you attempt to catch a single drop at the center of the mess and not get wet. It's virtually impossible, I know, and the best course of action is to accept that there is no avoiding getting soaked, and you should simply let it happen. You'll deal with the resulting damage in your way when you feel ready. Grief is more than sadness or missing the individual; it presents emotional, cognitive, and behavioral challenges that defy the social expectation of carrying on with life as usual (Szuhany et al., 2021).

When children pass away, parents grieve the loss of that child's existence and future, and all the hopes and dreams that a parent wishes upon that child. Parents mourn that loss until the day they die, and some parents never quite recover from grief. Lang et al., in the 2011 article Perinatal Loss and Parental Grief: The Challenge of Ambiguity and Disenfranchised Grief, explain the "disenfranchisement of the grief experience" (Lang et al., 2011, p. 3), that losing a parent or sibling can also leave you with a crippling sense of injustice, and you may feel very numb after the shock and realizations set in. You do realize, eventually, that you will never see your loved one again, and it takes a while for the brain to accept this new reality (McCoy, 2021). When you think about it, if you lose a partner, a spouse, a sibling, or anyone else, the implication is that you're part of a whole. Your sense of self, while previously bound with your loved one in some way, seems lost because you're one entity now. We have encoded in our heads "we" or "us" when we are part of a couple or family, or in a very close friendship. Now your brain has to adapt to "me" and "I." The brain grieves this loss, and the emotions allow you to process this new information (McCoy, 2021).

My profession as a nurse grants me a unique perspective on grief and dying. I still feel as much as my patients' loved ones, but my commitment to being professional tends to dull my grief reaction. I find that my professionalism can make it especially hard for me to go through the grieving process, as this learned behavior leaks into my personal life. Toward patients' families,

I will focus on my duty of care, and I will offer support as is professionally allowed. However, I may (by extension) deny my right to process a profound loss where that loss has irreparably altered my life and how I move toward some form of normalcy and closure. Please don't suppress how you're feeling after such a heavy loss. Society has the mistaken notion that grief has a timeline, once you've reached that limit it's over, and that a certain range of emotions (in either a sequence or short-lived bursts) is all one should ever display for fear of appearing improper or brooding. I've encountered this expectation, as have others, and it doesn't make loss any easier to handle.

GRIEF AND GRIEVING AREN'T THE SAME THINGS!

Did you know there's a difference between grief and grieving? I know, it sounds like the same thing! Blogger Berly McCoy, in How your brain copes with grief, and why it takes time to heal, lays it out in plain language. Grief is the emotional state that destabilizes us and hits us like a giant wave; it's very centered on a period of time and it's considered a natural process that accompanies loss. We feel it for as long as we live, and there are a variety of types of grief (Wallace, n.d.).

Grief isn't just one overarching type, but it can be divided into many categories. These categories are:

- **Absent Grief:** If you were the caregiver, who was likely everything from maid to cook to chauffeur, you might not feel grief over the loss at all. You're so exhausted that you cannot feel much for the loss you've endured beyond relief or acceptance. You see death as an inevitable conclusion after you've done all that you could do to help your loved ones (Wallace, n.d.).

- **Anticipatory Grief**: This is the type of grief that is felt even before your loved one dies, simply because you know it's going to happen. This response is usually based on a terminal diagnosis or acute conditions that will culminate in your loved one's death. This is normal. Just knowing your loved one is about to die can be enough to trigger a grief reaction even before they take their final breath. Your body is preparing you for this impending loss (Wallace, n.d.).

- **Abbreviated Grief:** This kind of grief is very short-lived, mostly because one feels they must move on quickly and go about life as normal. They would rather not dwell in the pain, and very likely there was little to no attachment to the deceased individual (Wallace, n.d.).

- **Collective Grief:** Experienced by groups of people or whole communities, this grief classification comes about as the result of events like shootings, stabbings, or any other community-destabilizing event. The feelings are intense and shifting, and the community mourns the loss as a whole (Wallace, n.d.).

- **Cumulative Grief:** This grief category is thinly veiled as developing normalcy over death and loss, derived from experiencing a series of losses in one's life. In this state, the sufferer can find themselves feeling hopeless. The pain builds up over time, from one loss to the next, and it isn't until you've gone a long time without more loss that you start to grieve the death of a loved one. It's important to know that the loss isn't always just death, but it can include events such as subsequent job losses, loss of contact with others (as it was during the pandemic), or other similarly disruptive events in life (Wallace, n.d.).

- **Complicated Grief:** This is the kind of grief that is also known as prolonged or traumatic grief and is a diagnosis that a medical doctor is qualified to declare because of its debilitating nature. This is because it can look like depression, and you may feel unworthy or suicidal. Complicated grief is treated like a disorder, though, and medications may be administered to help you navigate this difficult time and lessen the impact of the soul-sucking pain associated with this category. It might be too hard to accept the death of your loved one, and you may feel deep sadness for years on end (Wallace, n.d.).

- **Chronic Grief:** This kind of grief closely resembles complicated grief. Complicated grief was first called chronic grief, and with this type, the pain of grief doesn't lessen over time (Wallace, n.d.).

- **Delayed Grief:** This type of grief comes about as a response to being taught that grieving is frowned upon by others. Perhaps you feel you should have already grieved the loss of that individual, or you would much rather avoid dealing with the loss. It can feel like it's somehow wrong to be sad or upset over losing a loved one, or maybe you just don't feel ready to cope with this painful event. You might believe if you don't feel it or acknowledge the death, then it can't insert itself into your life (Wallace, n.d.).

- **Distorted Grief:** This category is grief that is stuck in anger. The individual is angry at everything (i.e., the world, themselves, and other people) while they engage in aggressive behavior, carry open hostility toward the event, and may even engage in self-harm as a way to manage the pain of unaddressed grief (Wallace, n.d.).

- **Disenfranchised Grief:** This kind of grief is seriously unsettling because it feels like the right to grieve has been taken from you. Whether it's those close to you or society in general, by not being allowed to feel that loss, no matter how small, your anger and frustration can mount in the process. Reasons for being denied this most basic right can be as simple as not being cleared to take time off work to get through the pain, or you feel lost as to whom you can approach, and what you're allowed to say about your grief (Wallace, n.d.).

- **Exaggerated Grief:** To be stuck in this form of grief is much like living in a prison that amplifies all the pain associated with loss. This state of amplified feeling can cause the appearance of psychiatric illnesses, and even the development of phobias derived from hyper-grief (Wallace, n.d.).

- **Inhibited Grief:** Inhibited grief occurs when someone does grieve the loss of someone close to them, but it doesn't seem congruent with the depth of their relationship. They grieve, but not at the level people expect to see. You might see masking or delayed grief play out in this state (Wallace, n.d.).

- **Masked Grief:** This type of grief is found most readily among men in our society and is primarily due to toxic masculinity. Society frowns upon a man expressing his emotions, no matter how integral to his healing it may be. As a result, he doesn't show how he feels or share his thoughts on the matter. He shuts it down and pretends as though it didn't happen. The reality is anyone can land in this hot mess. It might be too painful to wear your heart on your sleeve, so you act as though life is normal and "fine" (Wallace, n.d.).

- **Normal Grief:** This is uncomplicated grief that can last up to, or slightly more than, two years, and it involves someone very dear to you. People want to put a timeline on this form of grief, but that just isn't possible. Everyone grieves differently. Normal grief lasts as long as is right for the surviving friends and families on an individual level (Wallace, n.d.).

- **Traumatic Grief:** This classification belongs in the zone of sudden or unexpected death. Tragedy colors this experience, and occasionally a person will develop anxiety, fear, and a whole range of unsettling reactions to startling events (Wallace, n.d.).

Grieving is what happens when we have to adapt to life without that special person around anymore, and we tend to carry that absence with us for all time. Grieving changes over time, and after a while, we feel it and recognize its presence. We know we'll get through this wave and carry on (McCoy, 2021).

Grief is tied to many of your brain functions, from memory recall to being able to see another person's perspective, to regulating your heart rhythm and the experience of pain and suffering (McCoy, 2021).

McCoy also discusses Prolonged Grief Disorder (PGD). This disorder makes it impossible to function daily, even if one wants to. They may forget to feed the kids or walk the dog, or they may even fight to get out of bed at all, letting all of their responsibilities drop in the process (McCoy, 2021). They may have a litany of thoughts rotating through their heads; they replay a series of would've, could've, and should've thoughts, and it spirals uncontrollably in this dysfunctional state. Therapists refer to these thoughts as "counterfactuals" (McCoy, 2021). The problem, however, is that the scenarios they imagine almost always end with the loved one not dying. This hinders a person's ability to accept the loss and in dealing with the reality they have been presented with (McCoy, 2021). Notably, McCoy says that, statistically, less than 10% of mourning individuals suffer PGD, while 90% suffer an exceptionally difficult grieving process without PGD playing a role. In this situation, psychiatric help may put people back on the path to recovery (McCoy, 2021).

26

In Memory of:
Kathleen Carroll
October 1937– June
2015

"Our grief is as individual as our lives."
-Elizabeth Kubler Ross (1926-2004)

CHAPTER 2

Children and
Adolescents
GRIEVE
DIFFERENTLY.

When kids of preschool age and younger lose a loved one, they don't yet understand permanence of this magnitude. They typically are of the understanding that death is temporary, and that it can be reversed. They learn this through their television viewing, usually, or even through the stories read to them. When characters die, they magically return to life and carry on (Grief and Children, 2018).

Kids about five to nine years old begin to process death and loss like that of an adult, but they tend to think that death won't touch them or those that they love. If the deceased was a sibling or parent, they often feel left adrift because others in the family, or those close to the family, are mired in the grief of their own and are unable to help care for the children. This unavailable state only makes it harder for the kids to process what's happened (Grief and Children, 2018).

For children of this age, it's perfectly normal for their emotions to go from one extreme to the next, and also for them to believe that the deceased is still alive. They can only remain in denial and avoidance for so long before it becomes detrimental to their recovery efforts. This prolonged state will only lead to further issues requiring therapy to overcome (Grief and Children, 2018).

HOW DOES A CHILD UNDERSTAND AND COPE WITH DEATH?

I met a woman, Allison, in my grief counseling group quite some time ago. She spoke about her father's passing and recalled a particularly jarring moment. Her then-sixteen-year-old daughter automatically started the trek from her school to the hospital, where Allison's father lay in the CCU. He had been there for a few weeks by this time. She got halfway there before she stopped, realizing in a moment of shock that he had passed that early morning. Allison had been present when he took his last breath. The teenager was hit with a wave of sadness that left her quite numb. She proceeded home that afternoon with that stark realization front and center, and she went through the motions of everyday life. I'm not certain that she had grieved completely, but she certainly had the grasp of permanence in death.

Later in Allison's story, she mentioned the passing of her husband's great-grandmother. Allison's daughter decided to stay home because it was too much to handle for her, but the two youngest went along for the trip out-of-state. When the family visited Double G (the moniker adopted by their family) in Palliative Care, emotion got the best of Allison's seven-year-old son. "Adam," she explained, "is a highly emotional, empathetic, and sympathetic boy." She remembered the tension in the room, the quiet words, and the sight of her middle child in tears and sobbing. Her youngest, five years old, was merely quiet but not nearly as outwardly emotional. It can be surmised that the youngest wasn't sure how to process this third loss. All in all, the previous couple of years had been tough for all of them, and Allison wondered if these events produced

31

long-lasting harm in her children. Leave it to a parent to think they have scarred their children for life through events out of anyone's control, right? Many parents, while amid their grief process, worry automatically about how death has affected their offspring.

Death is hard, it's unfathomable, and it leaves scars. It's hard to discuss calmly with a child or adolescent because that conversation has to be tailored to that child's age and stage of development. When you think about an adult's understanding of death and dying, it can be hard to simplify those thought processes to help a child understand the gravity of death.

Let's take it down to basics. Children see death through the TV lens or another medium, often in a simplified, implied fashion (for properly rated television shows and movies). It's important to convey to them that the reality of death is different for everyone and that their favorite characters, shows, or games don't necessarily reflect what death looks like (Jones, 1985). In Developmental Understanding of Death and Grief Among Children During the COVID-19 Pandemic: Application of Bronfenbrenner's Bioecological Model, an article featured on the Frontiers in Psychiatry website, Chachar et al. emphasized that no matter a child's developmental stage, children strive to make sense of death and loss. While this article focuses on COVID-19 related death, the material is applicable on many levels. Kids "may not have [the] coping skills needed to manage their grief in constructive ways to identify, normalize, and express their responses to [death]" (Chachar et al., 2021). In short, they express the vital component of a child being able to name and substantiate their reactions, both physical and emotional. This is a massive component of grief. Children's environments affect how they interpret and respond to what's happened to upset their world, and they need a safe space to express those turbulent feelings and thoughts (Chachar et al., 2021).

When it comes to children and their understanding of death and grief, nothing carries as much weight as psychosocial support to help children wade through this disturbing event in their lives. What this means is, you must consider a child's death and grief experiences, their history of adult interaction, how their community and culture shape their view, and the losses suffered previously (Chachar et al., 2021, p. 2).

Uncertainty, fear, and anxiety feed death and loss-related emotional reactions. This is mitigated by a child's assessment and understanding of a potential threat, and what they believe about their understanding. It sounds odd, I know, but even a child's uncertainty about physical symptoms of an illness or disease, or even about the afterlife, can affect how they interpret death and the grief that follows (Chachar et al., 2021, p. 2). This uncertainty is often fueled by ambiguous information and by the complexity of the information presented. Fear does its best work under these circumstances (Chachar et al., 2021, p. 2).

33

No matter the fears and emotions aroused after the loss of a loved one, the way a child expresses grief can be deliberate, but it can also occur from out of nowhere. These grief reactions can create a response to anticipated threats and thoughts of a myriad of dangers. This is called anticipatory anxiety (Chachar et al., 2021, p. 3), which in turn can influence a child's behavior, cognitive ability, and emotional regulation, and disrupt their people skills (Chachar et al., 2021, p. 3). When they fear death, experts demonstrate that this is a conscious response, and kids may experience the feeling of a loss of self-identity, or they might fear more deeply for things they don't quite understand. This form of anxiety can produce unnecessary pain and suffering and understandably produce stress in the child's family members (Chachar et al., 2021, p. 3).

Death anxiety is an interesting disorder. This form is recognized by the psychiatric field as an unconscious and highly generalized disorder. With this disorder, one of two things will happen (Chachar et al., 2021, p. 3):

1. **Death avoidance:** They'll avoid talking about or thinking of death in any manner.

2. **Death acceptance:** This response is the most welcome of responses because it means the child is coping with loss, and they understand death's finality. This signals that they have the cognitive skills to grasp mortality and death, and this is considered a positive development.

There is a recognized scale of acceptance that psychiatric professionals and grief counselors categorize in the following manner (Chachar et al., 2021, p. 3):

1. **Neutral acceptance:** Basically, the child knows that death comes to all of us, even if we don't want or expect it.

2. **Approach acceptance:** This is linked to religious beliefs, as they tend to see that there is an afterlife that is better than the life that is left behind.

3. **Escape acceptance:** This one is worrisome, I'll admit. This kind of acceptance has the child

believing that death is preferred over life. As a parent or relative of a child with this outlook, this can also produce stress in one's family.

When kids understand the concept of death in the entirety of its meaning and connotations, it's thought that they will either develop a fear of death, or that fear of death will be reduced (Chachar et al., 2021, p. 3).

Finally, let's discuss the six levels of influence on the child that will affect their ability to process death and loss. This comprehensive breakdown can help you see the world and loss according to how a child might perceive such a painful event, and it comprises the largest of a child's most closely connected influence (Chachar et al., 2021, p. 3):

MICROSYSTEM

The Microsystem encompasses the child's home, and the child is impacted by the reaction to grief and anxiety that parents exhibit. It's also contingent upon a parent's education level (Chachar et al., 2021, p. 3).

MESOSYSTEM

The Mesosystem level encompasses the child's relationships with, and conversations had among their peers, a teacher's communication efforts, existing community support structures, the values that shape the child's familial response to death and loss, and whether the parent protects the child. This is most often indicated by observable parenting practices.

MACROSYSTEM

This community level is, in large part, influenced by careless journalism, cultural belief systems, customary funeral practices, and ever-present conspiracy theories.

EXOSYSTEM

The study Developmental Understanding of Death and Grief Among Children During COVID-19 Pandemic: Application of Bronfenbrenner's Bioecological Model was created to observe a child's death and grieving understanding during the COVID-19 pandemic, the researchers went further to demonstrate the influential outcome of isolation, restriction even from close contacts, economic disruption and shutdown, limited external interaction, and the reduction of accessible family income due to the health care crisis and loss of wages.

CHRONOSYSTEM

Again, as it's particular to the pandemic, children were likely affected by the travel bans, further secluding them from extended family who didn't live in the same city, state, or country. This signals a loss of family support when facing death and grief.

INDIVIDUAL CHARACTERISTICS

Finally, the influence that a child faces and is subjected to is determined by their age, gender, temperament, and resilience of character. Alongside those factors, the developmental stage of a child can dictate social, spiritual, cognitive, psychological, and physical understanding.

HOW CAN I HELP A CHILD GRIEVE IN A HEALTHY MANNER?

It's important that young children not be forced to attend a funeral. They may find it frightening. You can, however, help them create a memorial to honor the deceased with a prayer or a candle lit in a memorial of sorts. Perhaps you can review photos together, tell stories and share memories of the loved one, and encourage them to share how they are feeling. Bottled-up feelings can make grieving harder than the loss itself (Grief and Children, 2018).

Parents, watch your kids for signs of them having difficulty dealing with the loss. Once they accept that things have changed permanently, their emotions can turn on and off on a dime, especially when it's a day of significance, like birthdays, holidays, or any significant date that stirs up memories (Grief and Children, 2018). Surviving relatives can help them to cope by spending as much time with the child(ren) as they can, and by prodding them to express their emotions (Grief and Children, 2018). If the person lost is especially important to the child, that child may lash out in anger. That anger may be further expressed in reckless play, they may have distressing nightmares, they may be especially irritable and moody, or they may act out in some other way. Their anger may also be directed toward other family members. They may regress if this is a parental loss, such as engaging in baby talk. They may also revert to bed-wetting or make unreasonable demands for food, or they may demand lots more cuddling. They may have trouble falling or staying asleep, as well (Grief and Children, 2018).

When you're stuck in the middle of the chaos following the passing of a loved one, it can be very difficult to drag your mind away from the inevitable preparations. While you worry about things such as a life insurance policy, the transfer of property ownership, or even locating the executor for an adult's estate, children may display rapid-fire feelings, fears, anxieties, and varying levels of understanding according to age appropriateness. It then becomes important to tailor your discussion of death to help them understand the permanence of a person (or even a pet) dying. It also becomes imperative to communicate to them that all of their feelings and reactions are perfectly in step with this heartbreaking event. They need to know that they aren't held to a timetable for how long they're expected to feel these things and that there is no rush to "move on."

HOW ADOLESCENTS UNDERSTAND AND COPE WITH DEATH

In Creative Counseling Interventions for Grieving Adolescents, an article published in the Journal of Creativity in Mental Health, Dr. Marty Slyter explores death and loss through the eyes of a teenager while addressing the factors that will influence how a teen handles loss (Slyter, 2012). Slyter, a Core Faculty member at Walden University in the Clinical Mental Health Counseling Program, has been practicing since 1980. She counsels community college students, teens and their families, and adults. Slyter continues to act as Program Director and maintains membership with several professional counseling organizations (Marty Slyter (Profile), n.d.).

Slyter dives headfirst into this complex discussion, asserting that teens tend to feel more deeply when they lose someone they love, particularly peers, and this is influenced by their emotional stage of development. If they are at their peak of development, and they're forced to confront their mortality or others, you can expect their reactions to likely be extreme, sometimes brooding, and sometimes fleeting. With a particularly painful loss, they can develop Traumatic Grief Syndrome (TGS) (Slyter, 2012).

TGS differs from anxiety and depression, the article stresses, in terms of decreased physical health, functional impairment, and increased incidences of suicidal ideation. This, the author notes, excludes existing mental health challenges before the trauma of death and loss (Slyter, p. 3, 2012).

With all of the above factors determining the kind of influence exerted on a child who is confronted with death and the loss of a loved one, it isn't difficult to see that what they see, hear, think, and believe can be especially confusing.

HOW CAN I HELP AN ADOLESCENT GRIEVE IN A HEALTHY MANNER?

Teenagers can be complicated adults-to-be, especially when they are forced to deal with the loss of family or peers. They aren't known for being overly chatty, though, and often sequester themselves to their rooms, or disappear to hang out with their friends (Simeon, 2016).

If you're hosting your teen's friend, and they've suffered a loss, open your door to them rather than shoo them away. They need their friends at such a tough time. Turning them away can cause more harm than good, and it's done primarily because death and grief are highly uncomfortable subjects. We rarely know what to say to those who are grieving. If the loss is within your family, there are things you can do for your teenager to make grieving a little easier to get through. Remember, they don't get over losing someone; they learn to wade through the process and to reach out in a way that is comfortable for them (Simeon, 2016).

Foremost, teens want to feel normal and don't want to be singled out. Daily routines can help keep their grief in check, but make sure to allow ample time for them to see their friends. Seclusion at such a horrible time will not benefit a teenager in any way. Their peers are their sounding boards. They will more readily lean on their peers than on Mom, Dad, or any other close family member. At this stage in their development, they are peer-centered (Simeon, 2016).

Let your teen take the lead when it comes to opening lines of communication. They want to avoid being told how to feel, what to say, or what to do. If you try to force a conversation, there's an excellent chance you'll be talking to a brick wall, or they will lash out in anger for being cornered (Simeon, 2016).

"Each moment contains a
hundred messages from God.
To every cry of "Oh God"
He answers a hundred times
"I am here""
- Rumi

Chapter 3
Getting Through
THE FORMALITIES AND WHAT FOLLOWS

You've lost someone close to your heart, or maybe their passing has left things unsaid. Perhaps you want them to know of residual resentment, or to thank them for their influence in your life. Your mind probably feels like it's stuck in a cyclone, spinning so forcefully that your thoughts, actions, and emotions just feel too tumultuous for you to make any sense of the entire mess. When someone passes on, it takes a lot out of us and makes it hard to focus on anything of importance.

You do hit a sort of "flat line" when it comes time to do the heavy, heartrending work of laying someone to rest and providing a fitting tribute to the life they led. You likely want to provide a service or memorial that your loved one would approve of. This, inadvertently, can open you up to the funeral provider's sales tactics and draining what exists of family finances.

43

Allison and I spoke of her experience following one particular grief counseling group session, from when she'd lost her father. Allison relayed that the funeral home staff "tag-teamed" her and her older sibling when they met to make arrangements. Their parents had purchased mausoleum spaces, and her father's space was paid for. It was at that moment that they attempted to secure another contract with which to "top up" their mother's account. All the money that had been put toward shared services had been funneled into one service, with the expectation that her mother would continue to pay the funeral home to keep her spot. They were trying to take advantage of a grieving family, using guilt and combined team efforts to get more money out of this tragedy. Needless to say, Allison and her sister were quite offended and upset after an already awful loss. These efforts, however, drove Allison's family to do as much as they could, under combined efforts of their own, to cut costs and still provide a suitable memorial for their father.

In short, be careful of professionals trying to bleed you dry. It's their job to get you to spend more, and they are exceptionally talented at accomplishing this very task.

If the responsibility is on you to make burial or cremation arrangements, walk in with open ears and open eyes. Be firm about needing a day or two to consider the options presented to you. Despite the urgency expressed by your funeral coordinators, there is no hurry. You can take the time you need to make responsible decisions and enlist the support of family members. This may be in your best interest.

MAKING ARRANGEMENTS AND GOING THROUGH THE MOTIONS

In my experience with dealing with the death of my partner, Amber, I wasn't allowed to create this celebration of life because Amber's mother and grandfather took the organizational role. They didn't see me as someone who should have a say in the arrangements since Amber and I were not officially married. I provided the clothes for her mom, who collected them. They didn't have the money to pay for a lavish funeral, so they purchased a modest casket and arranged a simple graveside funeral. They hired a young man to play the guitar and sing a few songs that they knew Amber liked, and I asked several of my co-workers and their sons to carry the casket. While mourning the loss of our shared future and aspirations, I felt like a mere spectator in the efforts to produce a suitable celebration of the life she led, who she was, and what she valued most.

Funeral Planning

There is plenty of organization and planning to tackle, depending upon the beliefs, preferences, and previous planning efforts set forth by the deceased or their families. Do they want a traditional funeral, a cremation with a memorial, a wake, or a more modern Celebration of Life? Moreover, have they already selected a funeral home and paid for a plot or compartment in a mausoleum? From known details, you can create a definitive list of acts that must occur and of the items that must be present, and you can tailor your experience by the budget available for the service or interment, or any other combination (Funeral Planning Checklist, n.d.).

Before you meet with a funeral home representative, you have decisions to make, and you need to be aware of any previously set arrangements. After all, you're endeavoring to honor your loved one's life with a suitable concluding ceremony.

First, who will be the main point of contact to be responsible for direct communication with the funeral home? Have you figured out who will be present to support you in this very hard time? This person can be a close friend or a member of the family, and their job is to be present when you confer with the funeral home. They will also be expected to take detailed notes, so that nothing is forgotten or left out (Funeral Planning Checklist, n.d.).

Find out what, if anything, has already been paid for and arranged. This could mean that your loved one already has a burial plot, an urn, or a space for that urn in the mausoleum (Funeral Planning Checklist, n.d.). Did your loved one leave anything in writing as per preference?

Finally, don't forget to have on hand for the conference your loved one's will (if it's available or even exists), life insurance policies, and their Social Insurance Number (either via card or on a taxation document) (Funeral Planning Checklist, n.d.).

You will be asked about what service elements are to be present. This alludes to any important religious rites as being culturally specific or traditional in any way. You will be asked if this funeral is faith-based, non-denominational, or non-religious in nature. Perhaps your loved one wants their cremation remains to go up in a fiery display of bright fireworks, or some other imaginative measure. These services are entirely individual but be certain whatever you set into motion follows the letter of the law. These laws can differ from state to state and country to country (Funeral Planning Checklist, n.d.).

In summary, on the day of your conference with the funeral home director and staff, you'll need to bring (if applicable) the following items (Funeral Planning Checklist, n.d.):

- Viewing clothing, or perhaps there is a special outfit that is preferred for the service. Factors like whether it's a cremation or casket burial will dictate what is appropriate.

- Eyeglasses or jewelry (keeping in mind that in some cases these items will be sent with the deceased or returned to you upon completion of the interment.

- A recent photo of your loved one (for cosmetic purposes if an open casket viewing is to be planned).

- Make sure you have the Social Insurance and Life Insurance policy documents on hand.

- If you have decided to do a traditional burial, do you have contact information for six to eight pallbearers? If not, start asking now. The sooner you have confirmed pallbearers, the easier the process will be.

- Gather a collection of about thirty photos to create a digital archive and multimedia scrapbook. Many funeral homes will create a page on which loved ones can leave messages, make donations in honor of the deceased, or even provide an address where flowers can be delivered prior to the service. The technological age we live in makes it easy to connect from great distances, so use this feature to take some of the work off your hands.

47

- You need to get a copy of the official death certificate. To get this item, you need the following details with which to complete the process (Funeral Planning Checklist, n.d.).:

  - The deceased's full legal name.

  - The deceased's Social Insurance Number (and documented proof).

  - The deceased's date of birth and date of death.

  - The deceased's last known address and time of death.

  - The deceased's marital status, and if they were married, the name of the surviving spouse (full legal name).

- The deceased's father's full legal name.

- The deceased's mother's full legal name and maiden name.

- The deceased's location when they died (i.e., city and state).

- The deceased's highest achieved level of education and what they did for a living before they passed on.

Don't forget to talk to your local veterans' offices if your loved one served in the armed forces, Emergency Services, or any other monumental public service organization at any point in their life. Veterans may arrive at the service as a group and honor the passing of one of their own. In Allison's experience, the local Legion created a touching procession where veterans each pinned a poppy to a company blanket, uttering words of farewell to mark the occasion. She recalls it being a slow procession, one at a time, and supremely heartfelt. The blanket was then ceremonially presented to Allison's mother.

Detailing the plans is perhaps the most painful part of processing that loved one's passing, next to (if applicable) paying for the service, materials, and any other associated fees. Funerals and cremations can be very costly.

If you need to subsidize the costs, try looking into your local university's Anatomical Gifts program. This is also an option often expressed in the deceased's preferences. In some instances, when the body is accepted (by an application created before death), arrangements are made to pick up the body and transport it back to the medical faculty location. The University may most likely cover the costs of cremation and later return the ashes to you a year or two later. Keep in mind, the medical faculty will use all necessary organs and body systems to further medical research or to teach our future medical professionals. This is somewhat like signing the organ donation part of your driver's license so that you may save the lives of others in the event of your death. Depending upon your religious beliefs or personal preferences, this may or may not be an acceptable option. There is no right or wrong answer, as this is highly individual.

ENTERING SURVIVAL MODE

So, you've gotten through the hard, very public business of laying your loved one(s) to rest. "Now what?" you may ask. Well, now it's time to allow all the complicated, painful feelings to roll about at will. Your job is to feel all of it. This is how we grieve properly. Bottling any part of it leads to unresolved feelings that later emerge to disrupt relationships, your own mental health, and well-being. Please remember that this experience is not solely emotional or mental. Studies have shown that grief also affects us on a physical level.

At times, a significant loss can trigger something we have come to know as "Broken Heart Syndrome" (Biteker et al., 2009). Plainly stated, a grieving person, even in childhood, can develop a disorder called "takotsubo Cardiomyopathy" (Biteker et al., 2009). Physical and emotional distress precede this condition, and studies indicate this condition is most prominent in women aged 60 and over. There are recorded instances of development in young adult and childhood populations, however, so please pay close attention to the state of surrounding loved ones while the loss is fresh, and further down the line (Biteker et al., 2009).

Did you know there are neurological studies that dig deep into the mechanics of Survival Mode following grief? According to Dr. Lisa Schulman, a neurologist at the Maryland School of Medicine, your brain views grief as an actual survival threat, provoking a stress response that is called "fight-or-flight." This, she states, activates the fear center—your amygdala (Hrvatin, 2021). Shulman extols that the brain perceives the loss of a loved one as a threat to survival, triggering a stress response known as fight or flight and strengthening the fear center of the brain. At the same time, connections between this part of the brain and the advanced brain—which is responsible for logic and reasoning—become weakened. In other words, the fear center of our brain takes over (Hrvatin, 2021).

Simple things like looking at photos, hearing a favorite song, or even having a conversation that reminds you of the loss in the most casual of settings can trigger a fight-or-flight response. The fear center steers your life in this awful time, sending you into unpredictable waves of grief that leave you feeling this exaggerated stress response...until you've gotten through survival mode to the point of rewiring, where fear no longer controls your grief reactions. It really helps to know that you aren't the only one going through this; knowing others suffer the same damaging patterns is surprisingly helpful to returning your mind to a state of pre-trauma normalcy (Hrvatin, 2021).

You've probably heard about the five stages of grief; they are anger, denial, bargaining, depression, and acceptance. It's important to know that you won't go through these stages in any particular order, and you will likely revisit these stages again and again while you heal from the loss. There is no specific order for any of these stages to occur, and certainly no expiry or date of conclusion. You will experience these stages for some time, off and on, unpredictably, and it's hard. It's a painful reminder, but you will get through the grief to the other side. You have a "new normal" that you must learn to navigate, and it doesn't have to meet the approval of anyone else. This is your journey (Hrvatin, 2021).

Remember that specific components surrounding the death will determine how you grieve. How well did you know them? Was it a child or a sick adult? Car accident? If one dies of disease, you grieve a bit differently. Your support network, stressors in your life that were already present before the death, and even the way you normally handle losses will impact how you grieve. It's so much more individual than all the expectations of the world can ever try to dictate (Hrvatin, 2021).

51

Know this; anticipated deaths, while draining and full of upheaval, do provide loved ones the chance to take care of any arrangements that will be required, to set up the necessary finances in accordance with the sick person's wishes, and also to begin grieving. Sudden deaths leave a family stunned and momentarily paralyzed in one way or another and are usually quite traumatic.

When Amber got sick, I remember dreading the loss, and I was far from accepting it. Even when she passed, it seemed impossible. Speaking with Amber's mom after Amber's passing, she recalls grieving "in advance" for her daughter's declining health. She told me how exhausting it was, knowing that one day she would get that phone call. She admitted to me that the last night she saw Amber in the hospital, she knew it would be her last. She went home, turned her phone off, and prayed for Amber's comfortable passing. It's exhausting to know that your loved one is going away, albeit slowly and with a sort of yo-yo effect for some, and people tend to start the grieving process even before the loved one is actually gone. When that time comes, it's a strange sort of exhale, like there is a conclusion to a never-ending drama that allows both pain and relief to exist in the same space. And, oh, the guilt for not grieving as deeply as those who just found out about the loved one's passing. We hold ourselves at gunpoint when we don't seem to share the same depth of emotional disruption as those around us, and we berate our psyches because of it. It's a very strange state.

"GRIEF IS LIKE THE OCEAN.
IT COMES ON WAVES, EBBING
AND FLOWING.
SOMETIMES THE WATER IS
CALM, AND
SOMETIMES IT IS OVERWHELMING.
ALL WE CAN DO IS LEARN TO
SWIM."
- VICKI HARRISON

Chapter 4

Dealing With Panic Attacks

and Roller Coaster Emotions

I had never experienced a panic attack in my entire life. The first time it happened to me, I thought I was having a heart attack. I felt like I couldn't breathe, and I felt really anxious. When it was happening, I had a brief instant of knowing that I had to calm myself down by slowing my breathing. I took a couple of deep breaths, which helped slow my heart rate significantly. I then thought to myself, What is causing this? I eventually realized it was my grief that was the culprit. There is a reason emotions are described as rollercoasters when someone is in the midst of grief. They don't stay the same, and they are so completely unpredictable, changing on a dime with no apparent rhyme or reason. You know what? It's okay. It's normal. You're normal and experiencing a trauma so debilitating that it isn't possible to stay in one emotion for too long. Nor will you follow the stages of grief in any set order. You will switch between anger and sadness, acceptance, and back to grief again in any number of moments. You feel like you're going insane for being unable to control your feelings, and your reactions, and all of a sudden, you can't even catch your breath. It takes real effort to draw a full breath, to get past that invisible brick wall.

It's important to remember that while it feels so in the moment, you're not alone in grief. Everybody experiences this wild ride when they lose someone they love, though differently, or they lose a relationship. This is all part of moving toward healing. However, be aware that psychiatric symptoms can surface with the onset of grief, often in the form of panic attacks (Help Guide: Panic Attacks and Panic Disorders, 2019).

55

WHAT DO PANIC ATTACKS LOOK LIKE?

Panic attacks appear in the form of sudden, intense anxiety, and are often accompanied by a host of symptoms (Help Guide: Panic Attacks and Panic Disorders, 2019):

- breathlessness or hyperventilation

- racing heart or irregular heartbeat

- chest pain or discomfort (it can feel like a heart attack or indigestion)

- shaking or trembling

- choking sensation

- nausea or upset stomach

- sweating

- dizziness, lightheadedness, or feeling faint

- numbness or tingling

- feeling detached from reality

- hot and cold flashes

- sense or fear of losing control, dying, or going crazy

Panic attacks can come on fast, tend to peak in about ten minutes, last twenty to thirty minutes, but not usually longer than an hour. At times, they can last as long as, but not typically, an hour (Help Guide: Panic Attacks and Panic Disorders, 2019). They come out of nowhere, it seems. But medical experts will assure you, this attack will not kill you. Panic attacks are in no way physically harmful, but in the midst of an attack, you feel like you just might die (Help Guide: Panic Attacks and Panic Disorders, 2019). Panic attacks feel awful; I've been there. I understand how unsettling an episode can be.

WHAT CAUSES PANIC ATTACKS?

Nobody really knows what causes panic attacks in the first place, but there is a school of thought that extreme stress and life transitions have the potential to bring them on. Experts also note that panic attacks tend to run in families, though this isn't a hard and set rule (Help Guide: Panic Attacks and Panic Disorders, 2019).

Panic attacks can also be brought on by medical conditions, such as the following (Help Guide: Panic Attacks and Panic Disorders, 2019):

- hypoglycemia (when your blood sugar drops)

- use of stimulants (i.e., amphetamines, caffeine, and cocaine)

- medication withdrawal symptoms (such as coming off antidepressants)

- hyperthyroidism (when your thyroid gland is overactive)

- mitral valve prolapse (this is a minor cardiac issue that occurs when one of the heart's valves fails to close properly)

How to Stop Panic Attacks and Curb Anxiety

There are multiple ways to stop an attack in progress, just as there are many ways to put a cap on anxiety and its many symptoms, and the hold it has over you. This chapter aims to arm you with a strong toolkit to effectively disarm a panic attack and take away the power anxiety has over an individual. You don't have to feel this out-of-control every time a panic attack strikes, or every time anxiety rears its ugly head. You can take control, learn, and thrive with this new skill set.

58

Local Library Books, Ebooks, and Audiobooks

Have you gone online or picked up reserved books at your local library? Google a list of libraries in your region. If you haven't done so already, produce identification and secure your own library card today! Upon receipt, you will be able to set your own access code or password, and an online username to jump into the remote or live experience. Your library will have a wealth of information at your disposal.

A search on the Internet will undoubtedly reveal a plethora of literature to manage these stressful events, and not all books have to be signed out or purchased to be enjoyed. If you have little time to sit and read, audiobooks can make the job a bit less time-consuming and may be easier to process what is being read aloud.

ONLINE, PC, AND MOBILE READING APPLICATIONS

There are numerous applications available for cellular phones, tablets, and e-readers, never mind PCs at home. Bookswritten. com has compiled some of the best websites to read books for free, and they are (Chaterjee, 2021):

1. Feedbooks (www.feedbooks.com)

2. Project Gutenberg (www.gutenberg.org)

3. Open Library (www.openlibrary.org)

4. ManyBooks (www.manybooks.net)

5. Free-eBooks (www.free-ebooks.net)

6. Bookyards (www.bookyards.com)

7. Kobo (www.kobo.com)

8. BookBoon (www.bookboon.com)

9. HathiTrust Digital Library (www.hathitrust.org)

10. ReadCentral (www.readcentral.com)

Digital books are available for download in PDF, EPUB, Kindle, TXT, HTML, and RTF formats to suit your needs, but availability may vary across sites (Comparison of [Ebook] Formats, 2022).

ANXIETY PODCASTS

You likely feel out of control and powerless to stop what's happening to you. However, there is a lot you can do to help yourself in this tough situation. You can learn about panic disorders and how they present, as well as how to bring yourself back into a state of control. Remember, this is happening because your "fight-or-flight" response has kicked in, fooling your body into thinking you're in peril. These sensations are normal, and no, you're not losing your mind (Team, 2019).

For people who are prone to panic attacks, they should not consume alcohol, caffeine, or smoking, as these habits may exacerbate the condition. Also, be wary of diet pills or cold medications, as these stimulants can cause a panic attack to occur as well. But more importantly, what can you do to put a lid on your panic attacks?

Let's remember that the basics of human health include a healthy mix of exercise, eating healthily, getting enough sleep, practicing mindfulness in a way that works for you, and remembering to engage in self-care to manage stress and anxiety (Maselli, 2022). If anxiety is left untreated, it can easily worsen and interfere with relationships, life, work, and general responsibilities (Maselli, 2022).

Content writer Ashley Maselli of betterhelp.com provides advice on finding those podcasts that will best serve you. There are a variety of styles, of course, the most prevalent being coach-style (which helps you to curb anxiety, negative thinking, and negative emotions). In this podcast genre, anxiety coaches may be able to help you unravel the mess that anxiety disorders may promote. While they aren't licensed to provide medical treatment or advice, they can provide information about meditation techniques and lead guided meditations tailored toward anxiety and depression. Some podcasts offer personal experiences and stories, and they may feature expert guest speakers to tackle difficult topics like past trauma (Maselli, 2022). You can search for podcasts on YouTube, Spotify, Apple Music, or the Podcast app, and I am confident this search will yield more than just basic podcasts.

Some of Maselli's top recommendations include (Maselli, 2022):

- The Calmer You: Chloe Brotheridge, an expert hypnotherapist, author, and coach, offers everyday tips and strategies for kicking anxiety to the curb. She teaches skills such as building your resilience and increasing mindfulness in your life, and she advises ways for you to become happier and more fulfilled.

- Anxiety Slayer: Shann Vander Leek and Ananga Sivyer offer tools and tricks to help you cope with long-term stress, PTSD, panic attacks, and anxiety. They feature collections of interviews and conversations with psychology experts while offering solid strategies to help you take control of your symptoms. Vander Leek and Sivyer cover materials like breathwork, meditation, and muscle relaxation techniques.

- Your Anxiety Toolkit: This podcast is hosted by Kimberley, a marriage and family therapist. Kimberley provides the means for you to learn to manage your anxiety symptoms and squash stress.

Her advice and tips are science-based and can help you cope with various mental health conditions.

I will add, I have a favorite podcast of my own; Healing With David Kessler, where he explores loss and that awful sense of being stuck in one spot when we know we ought to be moving forward. We're held back by grief and disappointment, and Kessler dives right into this tough topic. He hosts special guest speakers, providing the platform for their messages of trauma and perseverance to reach a broad audience (Grief.com Podcasts, n.d.).

BREATHWORK

When you hyperventilate, you feel lightheadedness and chest constriction. The key to dismantling this awful cycle is to learn to take deep breaths through breathing exercises.

The following are some of the most recommended breathing exercises on Medical News Today that soothe the body and mind, and act as therapy for lung conditions like Asthma and COPD (8 Best Breathing Techniques, 2020). Try each of the techniques listed below to find what works for you. It could be a combination of a few types or one of the entire sets.

PURSED LIP BREATHING

May I just add, this kind of breathing technique has saved this woman from blowing many a fuse... This method gets the diaphragm working, increases our oxygen intake, and keeps our airways open much longer than usual.

So, how do we do this? You'll find this one exceedingly memorable and easy to learn. First, breathe in through the nose, fully. Blow out through pursed lips, extending that exhale to twice the duration of the inhale until you've exhaled completely. Repeat as often as needed until you feel less agitated.

DIAPHRAGMATIC BREATHING

This kind of breathing, also called Belly Breathing, is great for stress and anxiety. First, relax your neck and shoulders so your diaphragm will do most of the work. Set your hands lightly on your belly. Breathe in through the nose, fully inhaling, and feel that belly rise. Breathe out fully through the mouth, extending that exhale to twice the time it took to inhale. Repeat until you feel you've done enough. Three to four cycles usually do it for me.

63

MINDFUL BREATHING

This breathing style entails full concentration on your breath. This is also a form of meditation. By focusing on the natural breathing pattern in and out, you don't change a thing. This, in turn, may slow your breathing.

Find a quiet place that has no distractions and sit or lie down comfortably. Listen to your body inhale and exhale. Let your thoughts pass without any judgment or analysis. You are only focusing on the breath sounds. Repeat this one as often as you need in your session.

DEEP BREATHING

This style can lower your heart rate, calming your body and mind as a result. The technique is simple and effective.

Sit comfortably and relax your shoulders. Inhale slowly to fill your lungs to capacity. Slowly exhale to empty your lungs completely. Each breath in and out should be done to a four-count for best results.

BOX BREATHING (SQUARE BREATHING)

Ah, I love this one! Allison told me this is her go-to when dealing with her teenagers. When she sees red, she feels this one centers her more quickly and effectively than all the other methods she has used. This style slows your breathing, reduces stress, and also increases your focus and attention. It honestly sounds like a wonderful technique to employ when sitting down to work.

Sit in a comfortable position with a straight posture. Your hands can be palm-up in your lap or on your knees to force the upper body to relax. Breathe in through the nose, fully, to a count of four. Hold for four beats. Release your breath through the mouth, also to a count of four. Hold for another four beats. Repeat this one for as long as it takes to feel centered.

ALTERNATE NOSTRIL BREATHING

I have just tried this technique for the first time, and it's a unique approach. Focus is most definitely improved with this method, and it takes a little practice to get the rhythm and methods down.

Sit comfortably and breathe out fully before starting. Now,

close the right nostril with the thumb of one hand. Breathe in through the open nostril fully. Close the left nostril with the fourth (ring) finger and release the thumb. Breathe out through the right nostril. Breathe in through the right nostril and then close the right nostril. Breathe out fully through the left nostril.

Those were odd maneuvers, but it felt very deliberate compared to the other methods, in my opinion.

LION'S BREATH

This one might feel a little weird, but it's great for the release of stress and tension. Deeply exhaling relaxes your muscles. Ready?

Inhale deeply through the nose. Now, exhale forcefully with your mouth open wide, and stick your tongue out at the same time. Ready for the silly part? Yes, roll those eyes skyward while inhaling to stretch your face. Done! Repeat as often as necessary and pay close attention to how you feel afterward. Sometimes, peculiar just works.

RELAXATION TECHNIQUES

Betterhelp.com offers plenty of relaxation techniques. As meditation has already been discussed in this book, I want to focus on the less discussed relaxation techniques. Let's focus first on those techniques that can be performed at home, and then the clinical option (BetterHelp, 2022):

- **Tai Chi:** Tai chi features flowing, slow body movements. It's a low-impact exercise that almost anyone can do, and it induces relaxation while improving mental health. Tai chi eases stress and also fights pain. If you can find the time and resources to learn it in a class setting, check out your local Community League. If you can't quite manage that, Tai Chi videos of various skill levels are available for free online. All you have to do is search in your browser.

- **Yoga:** Used to lower anxiety and stress, yoga improves overall mental and physical well-being. There are many types of yoga, so it might be helpful to visit a yoga studio or search for information online. BetterHelp.com offers this site for more information to help you on your yoga journey.

- **Progressive Muscle Relaxation:** This kind of practice can help you take control of and manage anxiety and significantly reduce muscle tension. The beauty of Progressive Muscle Relaxation (PMR) is that you can use this while stuck in the middle of an anxiety or panic attack. If your anxiety is through the roof, a short session of PMR without interruption can bring you back down to earth. How do you do this? It's pretty simple. Begin by sitting comfortably. Start by tensing each muscle for only a few seconds from the feet up. Relax that muscle and move on to the next, in order. You should traverse from your feet to your legs, thighs, buttocks, torso, chest, arms, hands, shoulders, and finally, the neck. Don't rush PMR. Using this technique, try to focus only on the muscle actions and let your thoughts pass by. With enough practice, PMR can lower your anxiety levels and improve your quality of sleep.

- **Rhythmic Movement and Mindful Exercise:** This kind of movement is purely physical, and some of my favorite forms are walking, dancing, and swimming. The key to relaxation is focusing solely on the exercise itself and how your body feels doing it. Is there a rhythm or repetitive motion? If you're dancing, what does the music feel like? How do your muscles feel in all that movement? Think of nothing else while participating in this activity. Don't forget to notice your breathing. You're focusing on this moment and nothing else outside your movement efforts.

- **EMG Biofeedback:** Electromyography treats anxiety and is used to lessen situational anxiety (like the anxiety you may feel when giving a big presentation) or general anxiety. The practitioner places sensors on your body to measure your muscle tension. In turn, the sensors provide feedback via pulses and sounds.

Socialization

Meet with your friends and families to reconnect with those you love. Social support helps a person to feel grounded (Team, 2019).

Get regular exercise! It can be as simple as a daily walk or jog, yoga, or any other activity that stimulates your senses and makes you feel whole under normal circumstances (Team, 2019).

Get enough shut eye. It's well documented that inadequate sleep leaves us vulnerable to physical and mental health issues

HOW DO I HELP SOMEONE WHO IS SUFFERING A PANIC ATTACK?

First off, stay calm. The person going through a panic attack really hasn't a sense of time and feels like they might actually die. Your voice can calm them, and if it does, keep talking. They need to know the attack will stop shortly, that you won't leave, and that they'll be okay. Stop talking if they ask you to, however. Follow their cues. (Raypole, 2020).

Ask them how you can help. When they're in the throes of an attack, they might not be able to tell you, but if you know them already, ask before witnessing an attack what best works for them. They might snap at you, so try not to take their response personally. They're enduring "fight-or-flight" and really cannot keep a clear head during the panic attack (Raypole, 2020).

Do you know the warning signs of an impending panic attack or one already in progress? Let's go through the key markers (Raypole, 2020):

1. They feel a sense of fear or dread.

2. They are hyperventilating or appear short of breath.

3. They feel like they're choking.

4. They feel like their heart is racing or pounding.

5. They might be dizzy or trembling.

These signs aren't typical of every panic attack, so be sure to ask them in advance what a panic attack feels like for them. If you can catch the attack early, you can move them off to a quiet place with more privacy to get them through it. Before you move them, though, make sure this is what they want. Ask them. Carry on a light conversation unless they tell you to stop talking, and frequently remind them to breathe through the attack (Raypole, 2020).

If they want to hear you speak, don't be repetitive in your questions. Asking them repeatedly if they're okay can, in fact, make them feel at fault for not feeling all right (Raypole, 2020).

Panic attacks don't make a lot of sense to the sufferer or those around them. It's often an irrational response to something perfectly benign, either elicited by a stressful situation or even while they are resting perfectly peacefully (Raypole, 2020).

Validate their panicked state. Your empathetic response can go a long way to reassuring them that there's no need to be embarrassed, and you can acknowledge that panic attacks come out of nowhere. Just let them know you're there to support them without judgment (Raypole, 2020).

Try using the "five senses" grounding technique. Have them name (Smith, 2018):

- five things they see around them

- four things they can touch

- three things they can hear

- two things they can smell, and

- One thing they can taste.

You can repeat this exercise many times, for as long as it takes for grounding to occur

"Goodbyes are only for those
who love with their eyes.
Because for those who love
with heart and soul
There is no such thing as
separation."
- Rumi

Chapter 5

Contacting Your

Departed Loved One

Depending on your spiritual leanings and belief in the afterlife, you may have (or want to) connect with your deceased loved one or tap into the spiritual realm so that you can find a way to heal your pain by consulting those who came before us. Some people believe they experience many instances of strange events in and around the homes of the departed. Let me recount a story that, to some, may be frightening. I found it oddly reassuring, and even a bit comical. I have a couple of instances to share with you.

Allison, my friend from the grief circle, told me about her experience. A year had passed since Allison lost her father, and it was his birthday. She must have been preoccupied, busy with work and life in general. She settled in to take a nice, long, hot bath. She couldn't have been in there for more than half an hour when the doorknob started rattling. Allison immediately concluded that it had to be one of her children trying to get in to use the washroom. Of course, she bade them entry, but she got no reply. After this occurred a second time, perhaps a few minutes later, Allison quickly got dressed and went down to see who the culprit was. It was neither of her children, apparently, as they were deeply engrossed in cartoons. At that moment, as she ascended the steps, it hit her. She paused and looked up, wincing in recognition. "God, I'm so sorry, Dad," she murmured. "happy birthday..." She recalled that moment with a sense of shame, quickly adding that her father was not forgotten. She recalled that she was mildly amused, recognizing his personality in this event. As was probably his intent, Allison has never forgotten his birthday since! She still raises a glass to her father on his birthday, something I found heartwarming.

This second instance of contact occurred on the heels of the loss of my partner. Amber was born on the 4th of July. She

73

passed in March, and for her first birthday after her passing, I had invited her mom, Granddaddy, and uncle over to my house for a 4th of July party and a birthday party for Amber. I lived on the bay, with a pier outside, on which we would eat and convene in Amber's memory. The night before, I knew it was going to be a hard day for her mother. I implored Amber to make her presence obvious during the party, and I also told her it had to be pretty black and white, since she knew that I didn't always clue in right off the bat. Sometimes, subtle cues or signals practically have to slap me in the face! The next day, we were all out on the pier and dark clouds began to roll in, the rain not far behind. Granddaddy had already left for the day. Amber's mother, her friend, and Amber's uncle gathered inside my house. We were all sitting in the living room talking. I had an old console TV that wasn't even connected to the cable because I hardly watched it. Amber's uncle was sitting beside the TV, while her mother, and her mother's friend, were settled on the couch. I was sitting in a recliner facing the television. All of a sudden, the TV came on. I thought to myself that Steven (Amber's uncle) must have turned the TV on accidentally. Then the TV had black and white lines running across it, and then for a split second, Amber's image flashed across the television screen! Her mom and I were the only ones who saw it, but it was there and gone instantly. Following that boldest of signs, the television promptly shut off, leaving us in stunned silence.

I also believe Amber addressed my bouts of sadness with the arrival of meaningful songs on the radio, always at a time when I needed her presence. It didn't matter how crowded the store or restaurant was, I would all of a sudden hear one of "our" songs in the background. She still does this to this day.

You may have guessed I love to explore all things paranormal. There are many unexplained phenomena that occur when a person is about to meet their maker, and certain experiences that are connected to the deceased and witnessed by others.

Let's stop for a moment and ponder what it might be like to be able to connect with the dearly departed when they are no longer physically able to be with us. Science can neither prove nor disproves the existence of souls or an afterlife, but science has proven that our world, and everyday objects, carry distinct vibrations (The Physics Classroom, 2019). Put simply, this is because objects, though they appear to be stationary, are made up of atoms. Atoms are energy, meaning everyone and everything we encounter in this world has a vibration (The Physics Classroom, 2019). That is encouraging. People will shut it down because they cannot conclusively declare whether the afterlife does or doesn't exist, bringing into question our ability to interact with the dead. Whether you're religious, an atheist, or even an apathetic agnostic, the idea that our dead loved ones are still around holds a certain appeal and can be a source of comfort.

75

MAKING CONTACT: Is It Possible?

Death doesn't exist, according to Sheri Engler, a medium worker out of Medford, Oregon. She compares the life of a human being to that of a car lease. We are born, we live in our corporeal bodies, and one day we die, returning to the spiritual plane of existence. Engler reminds us that we are all made of energy, and energy cannot be destroyed—merely transformed (Oregonian/OregonLive, 2018).

I came across an article written by Dr. Elisa Medhus about her experiences with the paranormal (Medhus, 2015). As a board-certified Internist, Elisa was terrified of being seen as incompetent in her profession for believing that the deceased could communicate with the living, but she holds the opinion that it's the reality (Medhus, 2015). If a professional can make this admission, why are so many people closed off to the idea?

Whether you believe one can contact deceased individuals is dependent upon your worldview, spiritual belief systems, and whether you're open-minded. Do you believe in the afterlife? Do you feel as though your loved one is trying to communicate with you? Is it your goal to leave nothing left unsaid, and to seek the reassurance of these departed souls?

To determine whether you believe in the possibility, let's explore near-death experiences, alternate dimensions, energy and transformation, and the work of mediums (Medhus, 2015).

NEAR-DEATH EXPERIENCES

The Near-Death Experience (NDE) scale was constructed as the result of a study orchestrated and published by Dr. Bruce Greyson, published in "The Journal of Nervous and Mental Disease." In The Near-Death Experience Scale Construction, Reliability, and Validity, Dr. Greyson reminds us that people have been writing accounts of NDEs since antiquity. Note also that modern reports have been published in various medical journals, so who are we to say that NDEs aren't real? Physicians, psychiatrists, and other medical professionals saw fit to bring these claims out into the light for us to draw our own conclusions.

Greyson's scale is derived from a collection of responses to the study questionnaire and attempts to make such experiences quantifiable, even though they are qualitative in nature, and the narration differs from person to person (Greyson, 1983, p. 369). It's an extensive list, of course, and if you would like to view the scale in its entirety, it can be found at the following address: https://afanporsaber.com/wp-content/uploads/2014/01/The-near-death-experience-scale.-Construction-reliability-and-validity.pdf. The study is lengthy but eye-opening. Events like one feeling unreal and detached, subjects experiencing unnaturally bright light, as well as subjects seeing a mystical and unearthly being, demonstrate the variability in experiences. Greyson's scale just proves that no one experience can be realistically compared to that of another human being's and that the sights, sounds, and senses depend upon that person's life experiences and, to some extent, their belief systems.

ENERGY, TRANSFORMATION, AND ALTERNATE DIMENSIONS

Wendy Zellea, author of the article Death Is Not the End of Our Life Force Energy, is an Ascension Messenger, Luminary, and Keeper of the Divine Principles of Grace (Zellea, n.d.). Ms. Zellea describes grief as the "energetic and emotional withdrawal" of the deceased's vibrations and resonance from the Third-Dimension reality of the living. This permanent separation from loved ones is felt acutely by those left behind (Zellea, 2020).

Let's talk about how dying is interpreted by those who participate in energy work. First, as a person moves toward death, their energy does begin to transform. Their life force energy is moving toward another destination while the living body is less animated, less alive. Zellea tells us that death is not a mistake and is like birth. She reminds us that some deaths, like births, are easy and fast, while others are difficult and slow, and ultimately harder to handle. Death is, she espouses, timed perfectly so that no being leaves before their time is up. It's not unnatural or at the wrong time, but this is hard for human beings to reconcile—because we miss our loved ones when they die (Zellea, 2020).

The death process works in a way that we may not quite understand. It isn't the body that begins to die before the release or change of life force energy, but the changed energy puts the wheels in motion and the body follows shortly thereafter (Zellea, 2020). It's thought that the Higher Self and the subconscious work in tandem to set the conditions for a person being able to leave this world for the next. The way it's done differs, too. Some will take that running leap and be done with it, and others might stick a toe into the water to get more comfortable with the idea of stepping in (Zellea, 2020).

Long-term illness, according to energy workers, is caused by the erosion of life force energy, where the essence of the person departs slowly, and sudden death can be defined as energy departing rapidly. When we suffer from an illness, our energy drains temporarily, but it returns, and we begin to get better (Zellea, 2020). In short, the essence doesn't cease to exist; it transforms as it prepares to shift into another plane of existence (Zellea, 2020).

THE WORK OF MEDIUMS

Mediums are usually composed of those with pre-existing psychic, clairvoyance, clairsentience, and clairaudience abilities. Still, mediums can be trained through mediumship development circles (Mediums Know How to Contact the Dead, 2016). Clairvoyance is the ability for mediums to see images in their minds, clairsentience is the ability to feel and sense things, while clairaudience refers to a medium's ability to hear voices in their minds. They bridge the gap between this world and the next, between the living and the dead (Mediums Know How to Contact the Dead, 2016).

Mediums want you to know that your dead loved ones are sending you messages, particularly when you are going through a hard time. This is nothing to be afraid of. You might smell something like an aftershave, perfume, or even cigarette smoke when your loved one is near. You might have really vivid, realistic dreams where you see your dead relative. Here, they are usually trying to tell you that they are doing well and that they are nearby. Have you lost keys, or maybe a ring? Chances are, your loved one is demonstrating that they are close by. Mediums suggest you ask that loved one for help retrieving the item. Finally, you might just feel the presence of your loved one, kind of like a blanket wrapped around you in times of hardship. Many who have had this experience report feeling calmer and more peaceful than before they arrived to offer support (Mediums Know How to Contact the Dead, 2016).

79

I have had an experience with a Medium. I found one through a Google search, and I sifted through the reviews. I was very nervous and anxious right before that appointment. The Medium's reading left me stunned and thoroughly pleased. She told me things that she had no way of knowing, after assuring me Amber was present. Amber wanted me to know she was thankful for the love I'd shown her, and for supporting her throughout the life we shared. Amber wanted me to realize I had really done all that I could, and I could not have changed the outcome, regardless of what I did. She reassured me that it really was her time to go. I left that reading with such peace in my heart that I felt the burden and guilt lift from my shoulders.

To read more in-depth on contacting the deceased, be sure to find those resources rooted in scientific principles, as this might make the concept far more salient than merely personal accounts or theories (Medhus, 2015). The scientific community tends to dismiss things that cannot be seen or touched, but if that were all it took to shake belief, we would have dismissed things like radio frequencies and microwave ovens. Sound waves, radiation waves, and any other non-visible spectrum fill our communication, cooking, and vision needs (Medhus, 2015). If we had dismissed these invisible forces, would we even have our hands wrapped around the cell phones that you and I carry on our person for hours at a time? Our faith in harnessing this evolving technology has allowed us to push boundaries and remain in touch around the clock (Medhus, 2015). These invisible things enable our global society to function twenty-four-seven, and we cannot so quickly dismiss phenomena because they seem too far-fetched.

Some suggest that we raise our energy frequencies by concentrating on pleasant memories that make it easier for our departed to connect with us (Medhus, 2015). The next chapter will introduce the connection between vibrations and the ability to communicate with dead loved ones.

"LOVE IS THE WHOLE THING.
WE ARE ONLY PIECES."
-RUMI

CHAPTER 6

How Do I Raise My Vibrations

AND WHAT DOES THIS LOOK LIKE?

Author Karson McGinley, a life coach and the founder of chopra. com and Happy-U Yoga out of San Diego, teaches positive psychology and yoga. She offers a variety of ways in which you can raise your emotional and spiritual vibration. She defines a vibration as "the state of being, atmosphere, or the energetic quality of a person, place, thought, or thing" (McGinley, 2019). Karson reminds us that energy can be intuitively felt the moment it traverses into occupied space. Have you ever had a bad vibe when someone entered your personal space? This would be that individual's particular vibration, and you can feel the unsettled nature of their presence. Even Einstein knew that everything has a vibration or frequency (McGinley, 2019). Loosely explained, frequency changes with the rate of molecular vibration, resulting in high and low frequencies. If we feel light, peaceful, and happy, this would be considered a vibration on a higher frequency. The lower vibration frequency sensations can be described as heavy, depressed, and confused (McGinley, 2019).

83

Knowing this, let's look at Dr. David R. Hawkins' explanation of levels of consciousness (Saeed, n.d.-b). Hawkins possessed a slew of research delving into the field of consciousness. Hawkins was a nationally recognized physician, psychiatrist, researcher, spiritual teacher, and a favorite lecturer for consciousness students, and he sadly passed away in 2012 (David Hawkins, n.d.).

Some spiritual teachers refer to Hawkins' categorized description of consciousness levels and hierarchy, relying on Hawkins' studies and observations to help determine the optimal states of psychological and mental awareness as they relate to a state of universal understanding. The higher levels of consciousness, for instance, match our higher vibrational states (Saeed, n.d.-b).

Hawkins has broken consciousness down according to frequency ranges as they relate to oneself, using various psychological and mental states to explain the levels, from 20 to 1,000 (Saeed, n.d.-a). Nondualitylife.com author Saeed stresses that this is a new concept, but it does fall into step with wisdom tradition (i.e., Buddha, Vedanta, or Tantra) (Saeed, n.d.-a). Saeed explains that the higher levels of consciousness are tied to higher levels of psychological integration and to the balance of life. The levels of consciousness diagram is more of a map, showing us visually how we lift ourselves from our lower selves up (also called Small 1, a lower consciousness state) to our higher selves (also called Absolute 1). We do this by dissolving our conditioning and purifying the mind and body, allowing for a more authentic expression of one's true nature. Saeed emphasizes that this is not to be perceived as a new religion, as there is no need for this (Saeed, n.d.-a).

84

In this model, Enlightenment is regarded as a Full Consciousness awakening, and (again) is not related to Buddhahood or other Eastern Traditions (Saeed, n.d.-a). As well, Saeed imparts that, unlike in these traditions, Enlightenment is a state that anyone can achieve. There is, admittedly, some confusion over how the model's numbers are measured per level, but let's look solely at the leveling potential on a base level (Saeed, n.d.-a). Take a look at the table following

Levels of Consciousness Map (Saeed, n.d.-b)

Levels of Consciousness	Self-Identification	Category	Vibration	Location
1000, Full Consciousness	1000, Absolute Self	Self-Realization	Enlightenment	Heaven
900, Truth Self Ascending	850–999, Supra Causal Self (Consciousness Awakening)			
850, Divine influence / Love Union				
800, The Great Void	800, Causal Self (veils true self)	Self-Empowerment		
700, Awareness	700, Universal Self		I AM (Deity) Presence	
670, Non-duality				
600, Presence	600, Galactic Self (shows the Inner Self)			
540, Oneness	540, Planetary Self (connected to earth and humanity)		New Humanity Consciousness	Paradise

Levels of Consciousness	Self-Identification	Category	Vibration	Location
500, Inner Love	400–539, Higher Self			
440, Inner Wisdom				
400, Inner Light				
350, Inner Acceptance	200–399, Rational Linear Emotional Self			In-Between
310, Willingness				
250, Neutrality				
200, Courage				
175, Pride	20–199, Lower Ego Self	Victim / Abuser Consciousness		Purgatory
150, Anger				
125, Desire				
100, Fear				
75, Grief				Hell
50, Apathy				
30, Guilt				
20, Shame				

HOW DO YOU RAISE YOUR VIBRATION?

Do you remember your High School science? Remember talking about the building blocks of life? Let's look at ways in which you can raise your vibration—your energy frequency—for the best possible chances of achieving contact with your departed loved ones, but also to achieve greater positivity in your life.

Let's first acknowledge that every single thing is made up of molecules and atoms. How do we know this? Quantum Physics uses this very principle in evaluating the world around us (McGinley, n.d.). We know that energy resides inside atoms, for instance, and energy waves reflect light and energy, and they never stop moving. Each energy wave has its frequency and vibration—a signature of sorts. Low frequency denotes the negative, such as the heaviness of sadness, stress, and anger. High frequency has a very light feeling, comprising love, joy, and happiness. It makes sense that we want to vibrate on a higher frequency if we wish to feel at peace (McGinley, n.d.).

In this section, we will look at the many techniques used to raise your vibration for the world around you. This will include meditation, aromatherapy, movement, daily scheduling, decluttering, a mini life overhaul, nutritional overhaul, digging into your creativity potential, disconnecting from technology, Reiki (energy healing), tapping, creating or finding an existing community connection, journaling, music, affirmations, visualization, and learning to practice gratitude. These are fairly simple processes on their own, but combined, you will raise your vibration, giving out to the world the positivity that you want to attract to your life. You're putting out into the world what you would like to reflect back to you (Irvin, n.d.-a).

If this isn't enough to convince you, how about this? Raising your vibration will help your flow and flexibility to remain in the higher vibration states. Connecting more deeply with yourself every day will also help, as will making space for those activities and people that you love. Your goal is to find deep joy in every day.

MEDITATION

Loosely stated, meditation is a way of releasing those thoughts, feelings, and things that no longer serve our best selves. This means learning to discard fear, anxiety, or any other negative sense that you feel is holding you back from being a better person. When you meditate, you're looking inward, and you acknowledge that by looking inward, you can create or find your happiness, love, and joy from within (CITE). We also use meditation to clear out negative energy and to cap the sense of chaos that encompasses the human experience (CITE).

You need about ten to fifteen minutes in a quiet place to just sit with yourself in silence. There should be no distractions to break your concentration. It's here that you set your intention. What I mean by that is, you intend to let more light into your life, or to raise your vibration, or perhaps to repel negative energy in this session. Each meditation session requires your intention to be set. This will help you focus on what matters to you.

One method is to focus on your breath. While you establish rhythmic, deep breathing, you also become aware of wandering thoughts and endeavor to drag yourself back to solely breathing. Nothing else matters. You notice things, but passively. This state of observation makes it possible for you to objectively note changes in yourself, either physically, mentally, or emotionally. You will remind yourself also, when you come back to your breath, that you have everything you need within yourself.

AROMATHERAPY

There is a lot of evidence to show that, in both humans and animals, scents play a significant role in memory recall and emotional manipulation. Scents have the power to alter psychological and physical states, and they are dictated by experiences and physiological states. For instance, when we smell food while ravenous, it smells amazing. As we satiate our hunger through consumption, the scent becomes less appealing. In Effects of odor on emotion, with implications, author Mikiko Kadohisa presents a review of the evidence available to determine the power of scents to alter emotion and cognition. The autonomic nature of the olfactory senses means that the senses can be associated with a memory subconsciously. Additionally, Kadohisa discusses the ability of scents to treat psychiatric issues and reduce stress, but also to influence motivation. The limbic system is affected, which controls one's behavior, emotion, and motivation (Kadohisa, 2013).

This falls in line with the idea that scents can heal and promote well-being. According to the site's Certified Meditation teacher and organization founder, Jasmine, scents are also an excellent way to raise your vibration. Lavender serves to de-stress and relax, while chamomile, Frankincense, and Eucalyptus offer calming benefits. Peppermint and citrus scents (such as orange, grapefruit, and lemon) are purported to offer mood support and an uplifting sensation (Irvin, n.d.-a).

Oils can be diffused using sweet almond oil, grapeseed, or jojoba oil. Concentrated scents are diffused with oil to avoid skin irritation on application. Oils are commonly dabbed behind the ear and on the underside of your wrists so that, as the oil warms, the scent becomes stronger. If you add an essential oil to boiling water, the resulting steam can be inhaled from a safe distance (Irvin, n.d.-a). Alternatively, try using scented candles or incense to set a room's mood and increase vibrational energy (Irvin, n.d.-a).

MOVEMENT

Movement, as health agencies have supported around the world, carries immediate benefits in the form of long-term health benefits. For starters, movement releases neurochemicals (endorphins, serotonin, dopamine) and elevates your mood, promoting relaxation while reducing adrenaline and cortisol (your stress hormones). Your stress hormones promote increased anxiety and tension. I'm not talking about exercise involving great exertion, but more like tai chi, the martial arts, yoga, dance, walks, stairs, kayaking, swimming, and hula-hooping (Irvin, n.d.-a).

KEEP A DAILY ROUTINE

Routines involve a consistent set of practices and rituals, such as brushing your teeth before bed. You need to create a routine specific to a part of the day that gives your mind undivided focus on something you enjoy doing. A routine can be as simple as having coffee on the deck when you wake up, journaling in the afternoon with a cup of tea, or even disconnecting for the last hour before turning in for the evening. While you have these consistent, calming routines, you can still insert some spontaneous activity or variety into your daily routines. Your practices will change over time, of course, and you might even get rid of certain elements because they no longer serve you.

But in enacting routines that make you feel good and in control, you will be able to use this to help raise your vibration further (Irvin, n.d.-a).

Let's create a plan of action. You need to find ways to work a new daily routine into your life. Ask yourself the following questions:

- What does your best morning look like? What would make you eager to get out of bed in the morning, or at least allow you to wake up on the right side of the bed?

- Do you enjoy a particular snack or drink that boosts your lagging afternoons?

- Do you need that walk or yoga session somewhere during the day to level out your emotions and stress?

- Finally, how do you like to wind down after dinner or right before bed?

DECLUTTER YOUR HOME– DECLUTTER YOUR LIFE!

First thing, clutter does nothing but lower your vibration. Even the word "clutter" evokes a low-energy response. So, how do you cut clutter from your home? Let's go over the following guidelines (Irvin, n.d.-a):

1. Get rid of the material stuff in your life that no longer holds meaning or seems to bring your personal space into an uncomfortable state. Toss out the unused, unwanted, and counterproductive things that make

91

it tough to really relax in your space.

2. It's time to be unerringly honest with yourself while you dig through your possessions. Ask yourself if the item you're holding serves you in any way. Does it bring you any joy whatsoever, or do you have less palatable memories attached to it? You have to ask yourself this: If you could rewind your life, would you buy that item again? Is it a regrettable purchase? If so, let it go. It creates a much lower energy than you need just by having it in your personal space.

3. Decluttering doesn't have to be painful. Set aside a dedicated chunk of time, even just a few minutes per day, to grab a few items with which to start this adventure.

92

4. Create four piles for those items destined for dismissal; Repurpose, Sell, Give Away, and Donate. There's no need to throw something away if it's in working order, so decide in which pile it belongs. Once you place it, don't lay your hands on it until you're ready to pack it all up. It's leaving in one way or another.

That last step is a very rewarding action because the space just feels better when junk is removed from your oasis. You can do this, and you won't regret it.

Complete a Mini Life Edit

It isn't just items that clutter a person's life; we can include people and meaningless pursuits in that category, too. This is a great time to take stock of your environment, the people in your life, what you put into and wear on your body, your daily practices, your online presence and representation, and any other component taking up space in your life and your mind (Irvin, n.d.-a).

It's time to filter out and remove the "noise" to make space for what improves your life (Irvin, n.d.-a).

OVERHAUL YOUR REFRIGERATOR AND PANTRY!

Do you remember how you feel after eating pizza and overdosing on chocolate or some other favorite treat? You might have felt a bit bloated and heavy, and maybe you felt the need for a nice, long nap... This is what processed food does to your body, and thus encourages you to maintain a low level of vibration.

Try digging into a plant-based diet with plenty of whole foods and plenty of water; remaining full of the right foods and well hydrated can make you feel spectacular. This kind of diet makes you feel light and full of energy, raising your vibration as a result.

In Whole-Foods, Plant-Based Diet: A Detailed Beginner's Guide, Jillian Kubala of Healthline advises that people consume less meat and minimally processed foods for optimum health. This diet, she asserts, lowers the risks of contracting heart disease, cancer, cognitive decline, and Diabetes Type II. The studies indicate that this diet is a solid preventative measure against these diseases (Kubala, 2018).

STIR UP YOUR CREATIVITY!

When you were a kid, I bet you indulged in numerous creative pursuits, all without worrying about what others thought. As you grew up, you set those pleasures aside and jumped into real life. Now is a great time to get back into creative endeavors! When you create, you produce a flow, reducing your anxiety, bettering your mood, and lowering your heart rate.

Try knitting, crocheting, painting, singing, drawing, writing, model construction, or anything else that engages your creative inner child. All of these tasks produce a result, and then dopamine floods your brain. Your results give you that dopamine hit which, in turn, helps your motivation (Kubala, 2018). It just feels good to create.

TAKE A WALK ON THE WILD SIDE: EXPLORE NATURE!

Earth, where man hasn't wreaked havoc or exploited its resources, remains untainted and full of energy potential. It's in the trees, the ground, the wildlife that live off its riches, and even in what feels like less-polluted air. Walk at a leisurely pace or hike that challenging mountain. Feel all the day's stress dissipate when you connect with nature on its many levels, leaving civilization behind. Take in the sunshine because we all know vitamin D helps boost your mood, aiding in better mental health and a better outlook on life (Irvin, n.d.-a), and try walking barefoot across fresh green grass, also called "grounding" (Irvin, n.d.-a). This is the place to let your mind wander and to watch your imagination flourish. It's easy to be bogged down by the work-life imbalance that plagues North American society, to chase the next opportunity, or to hustle as hard as you can until you have nothing left for yourself (Irvin, n.d.-a). By connecting with nature, you'll notice an increase in the way you feel; you'll feel happier and at greater peace (Irvin, n.d.-a).

GROW SOMETHING NEW AND GIVE BACK TO THE ENVIRONMENT!

That's right, plant something! Or go buy a plant and allow its presence to brighten and cleanse your space of negative energy. It can be any kind of plant, even a cactus, but it's a living thing that needs your love and attention. By providing for this new life, you reach outside yourself and shed pleasant vibes on your green companion (CITE).

Have you looked at Aerogardens? I have them in my home year-round, while I grow produce outside in the summer months. Either way, I am the "Crazy Plant Mom," and growing things just boosts my mood incomparably. I feel more accomplished doing this than any other task I could be doing at the moment. It feels much like meditation in its own right, and I love seeing new chutes and flowers. Even if you're a black thumb, no insult intended, Aerogardens are fairly foolproof.

Have you a grow light you can suspend over a plant table? That works, too, and not only for germination. The various UV settings help those lovely babies thrive. Of course, when they succeed, you feel accomplished. It's a win-win situation.

DISCONNECT FROM TECHNOLOGY

I know, you've heard the rhetoric before; televisions rot your brain, and both computers and cell phones make it impossible to settle down due to blue light emissions. While the first one isn't technically true, watching something mindlessly does have a zombifying effect; I've seen it in children. Trust me, it's somewhat alarming. Now, blue light has been shown to reduce quality sleep periods. Experts suggest you put down the devices and read a book, maybe knit, or do anything else about one to two hours before bedtime, giving your brain a chance to wind down, so you can have a full, restorative sleep session (CITE). When you've unplugged, that cup of hot tea or relaxing music can do wonders to help you relax after a long day, with the added bonus of raising your vibration.

REIKI AND ENERGY HEALING

Reiki and energy healing are considered, by those who practice this form of detoxification, the key to changing your vibration. Using spiritual guidance, Reiki practitioners can scan your energy, they can clear vital pathways like arteries, they can detach the negative energies attached to you, and they can recharge your field of energy, replacing it with positive energy, and shift your energy into a higher vibration (Irvin, n.d.-a).

TAPPING

Tapping, also called EFT (the Emotional Freedom Technique), is a method you can use to reset your inner energy systems, and it helps the autonomic nervous system to dispel the negativity residing in our thoughts, feelings, actions, and beliefs. By physically tapping on pressure points of the body (meridians), you can ease the symptoms that negativity has wrought on your body through stress and anxiety (Irvin, n.d.-b).

How does this work, you ask? Sustainable Bliss Company Inc., a website for meditation and self-care tips and resources, offers expert instruction on how to perform this practice. Go to https://www.sustainableblissco.com/journal/tapping for an easy tutorial.

The author, Janice Irvin, walks you through the process in a slow, methodical, and thoughtful way to ensure Tapping provides you with the help you need to raise your vibration.

97

BUILD OR FIND A COMMUNITY WHERE YOU WILL THRIVE.

If you don't already have a strong support network, now is the time to find your tribe. The people you choose to spend time with should want to lift you up and keep you grounded, and they genuinely want only what's in your best interest. Make sure these people provide the positive influence you're seeking, as well as honest feedback. Your communities can be local, or even online, in a forum for intelligent, informed discussion.

Just remember, it can take a lifetime to connect with the right people, but those needs can change as your life progresses. The same wonderful people who support you now could later hinder your progress, or they may move on to find that which best serves their life goals. Those you've lost contact with could just as easily come back into your life at a time when they need you, and you need them. We often don't realize the shift unless we really think about it, and often further into the relationship or after the fact (Irvin, n.d.-a).

JOURNAL

There's something to be said for spilling your heart out all over the paper (or the keyboard). Too frequently, our minds are cluttered, and thoughts are racing with a million different things going on in our lives, and we don't typically take the time to sort it all out (Irvin, n.d.-a).

Journaling is a private, individual pursuit that I find extremely rewarding. My journaling efforts wade through heaps of tumultuous thoughts, questioning the beliefs of myself and others, and allow me to throw as little or as much emotional consideration into my session as I deem necessary.

For starters, pick a medium. Do you want to write physically, or do you want to type into a private, locked file? This depends upon your preference, of course. If you choose to handwrite, try picking out a bound book that speaks to you. Places like Chapters, Indigo Books, or even Amazon carry a fantastic selection of artful covers that might help you find your flow. This is something I've done for years, and the need for beauty has never really faded. I like a beautiful book where I can leave my words safe and sound.

By moving your worries from inside your head to your journal, you remove a lot of stress through the simple act of jotting things down. Think of it like taking that upset part of you, and temporarily flinging it out into the sky, you carry less weight on your shoulders (Irvin, n.d.-a).

You can use daily writing prompts to start you off. Try recording first those things that you are grateful for, what brings you the most joy, defining your ideal day and figuring out what it would take to reach that ideal, and listing a milestone that makes you feel most accomplished in your life. Perhaps define what self-care is for you, what stirs up your passions, why your passions are ignited, or what lifts your mind, body, and spirit. You can also ask yourself how you might best contribute or what you can do to give back to the world. When you feel good about yourself and what you've done, or what others have brought to your life, your vibrations raise further (Irvin, n.d.-a).

MUSIC

Whether it's country, R & B, the blues, or any other genre, music can help kill your stress levels and help you to toss that stress aside for even a little while. Do you find yourself absently bobbing your head or tapping your feet to the beat of a favorite song? This is raising your vibration (Irvin, n.d.-a)!

Some people subscribe to binaural beats to raise their vibrations. According to Irvin, it's an auditory illusion. Two tones play at different frequencies, one in each ear, and your brain creates its own "tone." This is the resulting binaural beat, and this is another way to raise your vibration by balancing the resulting energies (Irvin, n.d.-a). Irvin uses the example of one ear receiving a 120hz frequency in one ear, 110hz in the other, and the brain creates its own 10hz beat to fill in the gaps. Irvin also recommends that Alpha frequencies in the 8 to 13hz range be used to induce relaxation and cut stress (Irvin, n.d.-a).

AFFIRMATIONS

Affirmations are positive "I am" statements that you speak

aloud while looking at yourself in the mirror. The idea is to raise your positivity by kicking negative self-talk and uncertainties to the curb. Examples of affirmations are statements like, "I am beautiful" or "I am intelligent." You could tell yourself, "I am successful" even if you're not yet, but you aspire to be. Affirmations simply help us to see what positive qualities we possess already, but also those qualities that we want to have. We have to say it firmly and with conviction, like it already is true, even if you aren't quite there yet. Positivity raises our vibrations, while negativity lowers them (Irvin, n.d.-a).

VISUALIZATION

Let's pretend that you can barely dog paddle at present. Now, close your eyes and picture yourself performing smooth, clean swim strokes with properly spaced breaths, and flawless execution. Visualization, such as this, puts out into the universe that we want to become a reality. It isn't magic, but this positive exercise allows you to call positive changes into your life, no matter the challenge presented. Maybe it's that year-end presentation that you dread; visualizing your successful delivery will help you move toward meeting that goal. This, in turn, raises your vibration. You have to visualize it in great detail and make it as real in your mind as possible (Irvin, n.d.-a).

PRACTICE GRATITUDE

What are you grateful for in your life? Do you have a roof over your head or clean clothes? Are you working a job you love and making a healthy income? These are things for which to express outward gratitude. Let's take it a step further and define why you're grateful for all that is good in your life. This act leads to fulfillment, thereby raising your vibrations (Irvin, n.d.-a).

"WHAT WE ONCE ENJOYED AND
DEEPLY LOVED WE CAN NEVER
LOSE.
FOR ALL THAT WE LOVE DEEPLY
BECOME A PART OF US."
-HELEN KELLER

Chapter 7

Embracing Happiness

AND FORWARD STRIDES

With your loved one gone, and the formalities of memorial and the flood of condolences drying up, you're not sure what to do next. Well, you go on with the task of living. You try to pick up in life where you left off, rather unwillingly at first, and as a party of one. It feels surreal and unnatural, against everything you believe about love and relationships, and their conclusions. You're out of your depth, and it's all very emotionally confusing. Where do you begin?

In this chapter, you will receive guidance on recreating the future you desire by pursuing love interests or connecting with new people when you feel ready to step into the water. You will learn about the financial effects of a lost spouse, and how to protect your financial future. Experts provide sound advice and lead you into a more secure situation.

103

GIVE YOURSELF PERMISSION TO LOVE AGAIN

Moving forward can feel like you've somehow blown the conditions of your sacred, lifelong contract... but the contract becomes void when one in a partnership dies or leaves. When you're left and the other half moves on with life, there is zero guilt in setting the memory of that person behind you. But when they die, it feels like the ultimate betrayal to push that memory aside and search for someone who will make you feel whole again. There is no need for guilt; they would want you to pick up the pieces and go on with your life. Like any warm-hearted, loving individual, your loved one would not wish you to be miserable without them. They would want the best for you, and to be alone for the rest of your life would be a detriment.

This doesn't mean you have to forget them, but you have to accept that this loss has happened, and you're a survivor. With survivorship comes a responsibility to rebuild your life in the way that honors the deceased party and allows you to create a new existence for the good of yourself and your living loved ones. You have a responsibility to reach for happiness and fulfillment if that is what you desire.

Before you can begin again, you need to consider factors that may threaten to derail your efforts to rebuild, such as finances, personal guilt, fear, and the desire to perhaps find someone with whom to share your life again. Maybe you wonder if your baggage will scare a potential partner away, or if you're simply too damaged to succeed at being with anyone else. You might be afraid that no one else will ever measure up to the one you lost, or that remembering and loving the one you lost may be a sort of disservice to a potential new partner. So, let's explore these things.

In Give Yourself Permission to Love Again, Life Coach Ken Canion speaks of your worthiness of finding happiness after spending your life alone. In particular, Canion reminds us of the importance of going into this new endeavor with an open mind and heart, and with a willingness to declare your intentions aloud because failing to state your intention is essentially an unwillingness to commit to this new plan of action. If you're reluctant to speak your intentions, you aren't willing to commit, and therefore you have already decided you're destined to be alone (Canion, 2022).

There are stages that, with great consideration, will lead to allowing yourself to learn to love yourself again (Canion, 2022):

- Allow yourself to enjoy guilt-free solitude. You must remove distractions from this precious task because time devoid of television, books, music, or any other kind of distraction is time spent learning to love yourself. This is when you learn to sit in silence, to just be with yourself anywhere that you're at ease, and to get to define what you really want. When you love yourself, you get to decide what and who you want to allow into your life, and you will have your best interests at heart. Nobody can take that away from you.

- Give yourself permission to look after your body and mind! You deserve to feel your best. You need to eat well, get in a little intentional movement and exercise, get that all-important sleep, and pay attention to your body. If you need a rest break, take it. Don't push yourself to the point of exhaustion but challenge yourself to do better in progressive steps.

- Give yourself permission to forgive your worst critic; yourself. Serve up a little grace. Stated plainly, if someone accidentally backed into you, you likely would respond with something like, "It's okay, don't worry about it." Turn the mirror back onto yourself; give yourself support and patience in all things that you would allow another.

- This one is huge. If you're like me, you've said yes to far too many things that got in the way of the life you want. Well, say no to those things that will derail your efforts. Tell yourself, when you're at a low point on your emotional scale, lying around

105

like a slug won't do. Tell yourself that you need to pursue those actions and habits that will push you on the trajectory that you want your life to go. Most importantly, don't allow yourself to throw in the towel, no matter how hard the battle of the day is. Say no to giving up on yourself.

- That which doesn't kill you makes you stronger, remember this adage? Sometimes doing the scary things takes monumental courage, but these things ultimately help you to learn what you're capable of, and with this newfound confidence, you can fall in love with yourself all over again. So, do the hard, scary things. Face that fear and doubt, and just jump right in.

- We say yes to so many things that we shouldn't, do you know that? We say yes and triple-book our days without thought until our plans crash to the ground. We say yes to things that will burn us out, thinking it's in everyone's best interest. What about that vacation that you put off for years because it was too expensive? What if you really want that job you applied for? Say "yes" to it and find a way to make it feasible.

- What's harder than facing your feelings, you ask? Well, try asking directly for what it's you want. If you don't tell people what you want, how are they ever going to know? People aren't mind readers, and unless it's put out right in front of them, they'll likely have no clue you even desired that thing. Don't let the rest of the world decide what you're going to get.

When you voice your desires, there is power in that act! You will feel powerful, strong, independent, and immensely proud of who you have become.

- You know what's really tough? Exposing yourself to all those hurt and chaotic feelings. By facing up to them, and admitting their presence, no matter how hard the feelings are to view up close and personal. You will fall in love with yourself again.

- Take daily actions to bolster the love you're finding for yourself. With each action, like enacting a self-care ritual, you're reinforcing the importance of taking care of yourself and making daily strides to love and accept yourself. You'll learn to love yourself unconditionally, flaws and all.

107

- Okay, this next one may feel like you're showing weakness, but you aren't. You gain strength by asking for help when you need it, rather than struggling through a task or situation that feels utterly impossible on your own. With this act of self-love, you'll be able to reduce your stress and gain confidence by allowing your "tribe" to hold you aloft. You will, in turn, free up your mind to deal with other things.

- Have you ever done something so amazing that you were quite proud of your own efforts, and someone else decided to steal your thunder? Chances are, you let it slide. I really wish you hadn't, but this is where your inclinations will change dramatically. Remember that feeling of injustice? That doesn't have to happen anymore. Think of a time when you have kids or other young people in your life, and you've congratulated their efforts to do better at a task or two. Turn that mirror around again because you need to face the real hero in this endeavor. You have to tell yourself what an outstanding job you've accomplished! Soon you'll recognize your own achievements, and you will feel stronger, braver, and more in love with the person staring back at you.

Now that you've given yourself grace and permission to find your own way, you're growing ever closer to crafting the life that you want.

MAKING LIFE-CHANGING DECISIONS AND STARTING OVER

In a partnership where you perhaps shared your home and finances, it can feel very odd to suddenly be working solo to keep things afloat. The tasks don't end with physical labor jobs, caring for children, or providing daily care and attention to aging parents. It also includes looking at how bills and debt get paid going forward. The bottom line is, you're operating off a single income. This is where the difficult legwork takes place. You need to know your current financial situation, existing obligations, and a way forward when you return to life.

Before you can make changes going forward, you do need to sit on major decisions for a while. Psychology professionals will always advise that it's a bad idea to make financial, life, or career decisions while you're immersed in turmoil. Your judgment is clouded in your bereaved state. Major decisions need to be made with a clear head.

Here is an excellent example of nearly fatal mistakes made by Allison herself. She shared with me a rough time in her twenties when she divorced a narcissistic, abusive man, and she was faced with the prospect of raising her small child in a shared parenting situation, but ultimately on her own. She was subsisting on one income. She was scared, she was embarrassed over her failed marriage (believing it to be her fault), and she was at a serious crossroad in her young life. She remembered feeling adrift and realized something had to change. Unfortunately, she thought her job had to get the ax.

As you can imagine, this life transition caused deep trauma and depression, unfortunately, expressed in unchecked impulsivity. She was blessed that day, when her employer refused to accept her resignation, advising instead that she take time to think about it, and not to act until the dust had settled. It turns out, that job saved her from financial ruin. She didn't have much, and her employer turned out to be her lifeline.

109

While it wasn't the death of a loved one, it was the death of her ideals and the life she led until things ended badly. It was a transition that hurt so deeply that she thought a drastic change would fix things. Needless to say, she is now thankful for having someone in her corner. So, don't jump. Don't make that gigantic change, sell the house, or sell the car and move to Cuba in the heat of your upheaval. You could inadvertently be creating a brand-new path of destruction.

How Does My Spouse's or Partner's Death Affect My Income?

If you're a widow, there is strong evidence of increased financial hardship when one loses a spouse or partner. For starters, women tend to earn less than men in the workforce, a staggering 25% difference, according to studies in the United States about survivors of financial hardship post spousal loss. There are greater instances of financial insolvency applications because of the loss of income, which would probably be alleviated if Survivor Benefits were to become available earlier than 60 years-of-age (Fadlon et al., 2020).

As many will recognize, a single-income household carries significantly less buying power than a double-income base, and it's well below the median family income (Fadlon et al., 2020). The studies are based on wages, capital income, interest earned on investments, Social Insurance income, Unemployment Benefits, and withdrawals from retirement savings for the surviving spouse. Insolvency, another factor affecting financial security for the survivor, is due to foreclosures, bankruptcy, and debt relief, telling us that the survivor had an unpaid debt to contend with (Fadlon et al., 2020).

In short, the average household, after the death of a spouse, has not saved enough money before this loss, and the survivor is unable to borrow money to keep the household afloat. This is a sad reality that many people fail to consider, but this can be remedied with estate planning well before death occurs for either spouse and by both partners understanding the financial status and inner workings of the household budget and spending patterns (Fadlon et al., 2020).

So, how do we remedy this threat? We ensure our financial futures by understanding the household finances, knowing all the sources of income between both parties, and having an action plan to ensure there is no question as to how money is coming in, and how money is leaving the pocketbook. Quite simply, this is financial transparency (Fadlon et al., 2020). Would you be all right with your spouse having bought an expensive sports car without your input, or would you entertain purchasing a land plot without your significant other's explicit buy-in? Likely not, as such massive expenditures will impact a household's ability to rebound when finances get difficult. It's a joint venture to protect the household from financial ruin both in life and in death.

What Steps Do I Take to Protect My Financial Future Now That I've Lost My Partner or Spouse?

There are often hurt feelings and a sense of entitlement to the Estate holdings by other members of the family. However, if a will exists, this will supersede anything that the law would otherwise dictate in terms of money awarded to the survivors of the Estate. In short, an up-to-date will declaring all assets will erase any ambiguity over who gets what. Of course, if any party feels they have been unjustly excluded, they are free to contest the will, but very typically the will is the final authority over how the assets are dispersed to survivors (Lawrence, 2022).

The first step to protecting the survivor's financial future is to get in touch with a Financial Advisor. This professional can help you to identify all your existing sources of income, health and death benefits, and the accounts that need to become jointly accessible, but also retain accessibility following the death of a spouse. This preparatory step can save a surviving spouse so much anxiety and hardship and bring to light any deficient areas of planning. A Financial Advisor's goal is to set both parties up for wealth and success in both life and death, so a couple can focus on their future financial state and the survivor's ability to endure such a tragic loss (Lawrence, 2022). Likely, your advisor will have you list all of your joint and individual accounts, joint and individual investments, Registered Retirement Savings Plans (RRSPs), Tax-Free Savings Accounts (TFSAs), and any other holdings in one or both names. Then, the advisor can ensure that access is granted to either surviving spouse following the death of the other (Lawrence, 2022).

In the event of a spouse's death, the financial advisor will set up a financial plan if none exists. The immediate priority is, of course, to pay off any existing debts, and to ensure access to capital that has not previously been set up for survivor access.

Please be aware that all estates go through what is known as probate, which may significantly slow down the process of granting the survivor access to existing funds. Within probate sits the priorities of dealing with outstanding debts, and taxes owing from the deceased, and this can take a while to clear. During this time, a survivor may have to borrow from the bank or access a line of credit to be able to meet financial obligations and needs in the interim (Lawrence, 2022).

At this critical time, you need to be able to identify all income sources such as assets, pensions, health and death benefits, insurance policies, RRSPs, TFSAs, and unregistered accounts, investments, and undeclared bank accounts (Lawrence, 2022).

There are government benefits available for survivors of the deceased, meant to boost a survivor's income in the form of a onetime death benefit payment, a survivor's pension (monthly payment schedule), an allowance for survivors (also monthly payments) survivors (If You Are the Survivor | SSA, n.d.). Details can vary from state to state, and by country of residence. For United States citizens, please see this site for explicit details: https://www.ssa.gov/. For Canadian residents, please go to this site: https://publications.gc.ca/.

On each of the government websites, resources are available if you're in any way questioning the process.

Did your loved one not have a will before death? If so, know where to find it. If no will exists, legal processes decide what will happen to the estate holdings. These funds and assets may be equally shared between survivors of the deceased's immediate family, leaving the surviving spouse with less to live on, thus reducing the survivor's income (If You Are the Survivor | SSA, n.d.). It's very helpful for the surviving partner to be aware of beneficiary designations and for changes to be made (if necessary) before tragedy strikes (If You Are the Survivor | SSA, n.d.).

113

THE LOVE OF YOUR LIFE IS GONE, BUT YOU HAVE LIFE LEFT TO LIVE.

Yes, it's hard to imagine a life beyond your pained, grieving state. In due time, though, you get sick of feeling joyless and lonely, and you have a desire to get out into the world and meet new people or reconnect with friends and family, or to dip your toes into something you've always wanted to do. You know what? That's good! You can't grieve forever; at some point, you have to take the reins and move your life in the direction you want it to go.

It's Okay to Be Happy

You may feel a lot of guilt when it comes to wanting to feel better, to find happiness, after the loss of your loved one. This is normal. In this transitional time, it's normal for you to have a range of confusing, often contradictory, emotions. You may feel depressed and despondent in one moment, and suddenly, your brain flips to the idea that maybe now it's a good idea to embrace a new hobby or social group or to reinvent yourself. We tend to do that when we've suffered a heartbreaking loss. We find solace in redefining ourselves. You need to be open to all of these confusing emotions and feel each one of them. It's a survival mechanism, when the body has taken too much trauma and needs to find a way out, to survive this awful chasm (Is It Ok to Be Happy during Grief? | Pathways, n.d.).

First, recognize that this loss and the surrounding feelings are never black and white. You can be sobbing your heart out in one moment and laughing your head off in the next (Is It Ok to Be Happy during Grief? | Pathways, n.d.) It seems incongruous, doesn't it?

Believe it, it's possible to be stagnant in your grief state, to be stuck in that sadness with no apparent hope of escape. Many times, the grief will recede; something makes you laugh harder than you have in your life and then just as suddenly, you're slammed with a wave of agony and sadness. Remember, grief isn't static. Your brain is hardwired to save you when you seem to be headed toward self-destruction (Is It Ok to Be Happy during Grief? | Pathways, n.d.).

FIND YOUR SUPPORT SYSTEM.

There are support groups for bereaved spouses, parents, children, and even non-related loved ones, each group tailored toward meeting a particular need for the person left behind. The groups can be a source of solace and companionship, giving you the gift of others' experiences to help you slog through the painful business of learning to exist without that treasured person. You may be able to get such information from your family doctor, a counselor, a psychologist, or other professional service providers (Seeking Help and Support for Grief and Loss, 2014).

For those who are survivors of cancer deaths, your local organization's website would be a great place to start. There are supports for those whose loved ones have died due to suicide, violent incidents, accidents, and a range of other causes. The most important thing is to seek that support, connect with your surviving loved ones, and not keep all that hurt inside of you. Talk to those willing to let you vent completely.

THEY WOULD NOT WANT YOU TO SPEND THE REST OF YOUR LIFE ALONE.

If you had a loving, healthy relationship, your dead partner would want the best for you. They would want you to move on and rediscover life without them. That's what love is, wanting and doing the best for the ones you love and care about.

"How lucky I am to have something that makes saying goodbye so hard,"
-Winnie the Pooh

Chapter 8

Workbooks to Help

Process Your Grief

I know. A workbook seems like just another task on your to-do list, but a book such as this is a powerful tool in helping you come to terms with your loss and the resulting grief. In this chapter, you will find applicable workbook tasks that appeal to a person at almost any stage of life.

Dr. Adam Blatner, a psychologist, compares grief to an open wound. A wound will not heal unless it's first cleaned out, the wound edges are brought back together, and the body is given the nutrients it needs to heal well. When you clean a wound, you're removing foreign bodies, encouraging reconnection of connective tissue, and the wound is kept free of infections, allowing for optimum healing. When put into grief terms, you need to get rid of contaminants like unresolved guilt and anger to clean the house. This is called ventilation (Blatner, 2005). Just like wound edges are reconnected, the goal is to prevent social isolation from occurring by encouraging reconnection with other people, a phase that we call empathic support (Blatner, 2005). Finally, in grief, you have to feed your body and mind so that they get what they need. You need to foster a positive outlook on life to become healthy again, and this is called re-integration (Blatner, 2005). Just as wound treatment protocol heals the body efficiently, these principles will help you repair the wounds caused by grief.

VENTILATION

When we discuss ventilation, we are referring to the sharing of one's mental state, and this is especially important when it comes to mourning. Unfortunately, people aren't often aware of the support available to them to be able to release that pressure or social expectations of "grin and bear it" make us feel that it's inappropriate to share how we feel or what we are experiencing with even our close family and friends. If we bottle up how we are feeling or what we are thinking, this tends to define a socially acceptable strength, while sharing or displaying our pain is declared a weakness (Blatner, 2005). So, it stands to reason that we shy away from sharing when society is so unduly judgmental. When we find our supportive social circle, those who encourage us to be authentic in all things, there is room to vent, and therefore a better situation in which to begin to heal.

THEME DISCUSSION

Blatner works through a series of themes that affect how a person processes grief. In summary, he talks about the nature of death itself. Was it anticipated, or did the deceased know they were dying? Was there a degree of clinginess (did you cling to a loved one because you couldn't handle life without them? These are the kinds of questions he explores with his lengthy list of themes. These are important questions because they allow you to look at all the mitigating factors, both before they passed away, and the loss itself. Things like a person's role in the dying party's exit can affect how a person feels about that death. Did they get to contribute somehow before, during, or after the loss? This is the kind of scenario that can create guilt or resentment over something mostly out of their control (Blatner, 2005).

Depression can cause one to place a harsh judgment against themselves, like when we beat ourselves up over having not done enough to help the dying person. This turns into self-condemnation for the survivor, which is unfair considering the unpredictable nature of death's process (Blatner, 2005).

Empathic Support

When someone dies, the survivor often feels in conflict with themselves. While they recognize that their loved one is deceased, they still want that person back like the death had never happened. This is normal! Human beings are innately contradictory, and in matters of loss, we are no exception (Blatner, 2005).

Those offering support need to remember not to choose a side or "correct version" of events. Their role is to allow all emotional avenues to present themselves, completely absent of judgment. They need to put themselves in the grieving person's shoes to try to understand the vast array of thoughts and emotions that follow the death of a loved one. It's equally important for the supporter to recognize that parts of the bereaved individual will feel a multitude of emotions and have many stances. This person finds conflict with their dizzying array of emotional inclinations. The supporter is to be empathetic and to offer an ear, simply put (Blatner, 2005).

Re-integration

In this phase, your job is to reconcile the loss you've suffered with the way you feel, but also to figure out what your purpose in life is and how to meet that purpose (Blatner, 2005). Your sense of self involves the recognition and acceptance of your losses and redefining your identity. This is ideally a conscious effort where you, as the survivor, decide what you will and will not allow into your life. You need to identify what you need explicitly and seek ways to fulfill that need while remembering that your options have changed. So, you cannot run to your loved one, but perhaps another good friend is a fantastic cheerleader who pushes you to make healthy choices and to do the things that affect healthy change (Blatner, 2005).

One method that Blatner discusses is identifying the needs that the deceased previously filled, in as clear detail as you can manage, providing concrete examples. What did they mean to you? Spell it out. What experiences did you share with that person? And, finally, what did you mean to the deceased? These are great questions to address via role-play (Blatner, 2005).

In this particular model, you ask these questions from an empty chair and pretend the deceased is sitting right there in front of you. It's suggested you ask them the above questions. Then, as in Gestalt's psychodrama model, you sit down in place of the loved one, and you answer in a way that you suspect they would have if physically there (Blatner, 2005). In this way, Blatner proposes, you answer your own questions from inside yourself.

121

In reintegration, you're promoting healing by providing yourself with a sense of wholeness, by bringing those wound edges together, metaphorically (Blatner, 2005).

THE FOUR TASKS OF MOURNING

Mental health professionals encourage bereaved individuals to work through the Worden's tasks of mourning (Grief Reactions, Duration, and Tasks of Mourning - Whole Health Library, n.d.) for a holistic approach to healing the broken heart. They are:

- You have to accept the reality of your loss.

- You must process the pain of grief to move forward.

- It's time to adjust to a world that doesn't include your deceased loved one.

- Your job is to embrace your new life and find a way to keep your connection with the deceased at the same time.

Mourning is hard work, and arguably one of the most important tasks a human being can undertake. So, here is a resource for activities that will help anyone, young or old, to carry on with life after a devastating loss.

UNDERSTANDING YOUR GRIEF

Grief is a complicated monster. The following exercises might help shed light on your grief experience.

Let's get a clear list of the losses you've suffered. Start by checking off the following options as they apply to you (Jewell, 2021):

Present	Past	Event
⊡	⊡	Are you aging, or are your parents? Other close relations?
⊡	⊡	Have you suffered a traumatic loss?
⊡	⊡	Have you been displaced by a natural disaster or fire?
⊡	⊡	Have you lost sentimental items or were they destroyed?
⊡	⊡	Have you abandoned a personal gol or dream?
⊡	⊡	Have you lost your income?
⊡	⊡	Have you lost your reputation within your social, employment, or any other circles?
⊡	⊡	Have you gone bankrupt or any other kind of financial ruin?
⊡	⊡	Have you lost the ability to trust yourself?
⊡	⊡	Have you lost the ability to trust others?
⊡	⊡	Have you suffered a mental health crisis?
⊡	⊡	Has someone you love suffered a mental health crisis?
⊡	⊡	Have you lost cognitive abilities?
⊡	⊡	Has someone you love lost their cognition?
⊡	⊡	Have you lost your faith in a deity?
⊡	⊡	Have you lost hope?

This can help you pinpoint the source(s) of your grief, so be sure to note it all. You don't have to share this with anyone; this is an inventory of sorts.

ASSESSING PAST LOSS AND TRAUMA

Try to choose three of the most significant events from your past as related to the checklist above. Briefly describe these events, one by one. With each event, jot down what happened, and when it happened (date, season, your age, and anything else you can recall about the event. How did you react to the loss? You can use pen and paper or a word-processing program like Microsoft Word or Google Docs, and please don't hesitate to lock the file for privacy.

CREATE A GRIEF PLAN

For Children and teens, and perhaps even for yourself, this exercise allows anyone to create a simple strategy to help them to cope with the onslaught of emotion following a loss. They have a blueprint, then, for how to proceed when emotions or situations arise.

Your plan could look something like this (An Action Plan for Overcoming Grief, 2016):

1. Be patient with yourself and allow yourself to grieve. What are some healthy ways to let out all that emotion? This could include shouting or hitting a pillow.

2. Accept and remind yourself that you can't change what happened. You can feel anything you want to, but you can't change the outcome, and this leaves you room to heal when you realize some things are completely out of your control.

3. What people, groups, or organizations can you reach out to when you need mental, emotional, and even physical support?

4. You can memorialize your loved one with an online memorial page. Here, people in your life can leave messages of love and support. It might help you to see that you're not alone on this journey.

GRIEF JOURNALING

Journaling can help you put a label on how you feel while writing, allowing you to explore this idea as deeply as you dare. The best part about this method is this journal is yours. It is personal, uniquely you, and you have no obligation to share it with anybody. Journaling helps you to explore the depth of emotions that accompany loss without feeling like you are baring your soul to the world for scrutiny (Christy Kessler, 2018).

The other thing about journaling is that it allows you to reflect on your loved one, allowing you to dig deep into the recesses of the experiences you shared (Christy Kessler, 2018). You can be as mushy, detailed, and nostalgic as you wish. Your writing doesn't have to encapsulate pain; it can help you find the joy that's been buried amid the pain of loss. You can call to mind the things you did together, the things they said, what they loved, the foods they enjoyed, the aspirations they had for life, and anything else you can think of. Ask yourself why these things mean so much to you. There are no rules for what you write! (Christy Kessler, 2018).

This journal, for all its simplicity, is a great gauge for you to examine how far you've progressed since the early days of their death. It can be highly therapeutic (Christy Kessler, 2018). Journaling can also help you to release all the stress that has built up since your loved one died. It can improve your sleep, your mood, and even your outward expression of how you feel. Writing your experiences can help you process everything you've gone through in a safe, private place, without judgment (Christy Kessler, 2018).

First, though, let's decide on a few things. Does your journal need to be of a certain theme or a plain booklet? Do you need pre-set prompts that will get you thinking, or are you looking for a more free-flowing approach to journaling? Would a favorite or themed pen help you prepare for the task ahead of you? I will say, whenever I wrote in a journal (and I have for many years), I remember needing black ink. I don't know what it was about that color, but my creativity and thought processes seemed to flow seamlessly. But perhaps that's just me... Either way, journaling will help you dissect your moods and feelings, and to put the focus on something that needs to be addressed, possibly with the help of a mental health professional. Grief is complicated, so there are no easy fixes to getting through this difficult time. The idea is to make this time yours, and this journal, with all of its implements, equally unique and tailored to you (Christy Kessler, 2018).

Let's roll out a list of journal prompts to help you get started. These prompts will work well for nearly every type of relationship, and I encourage you to try this exercise. Remember, there is no judgment, and you can incorporate drawings if that helps you to bring your thoughts to the forefront.

Prompts can include the following starters (Williamson, 2018):

- The hardest time of day is...

- Today I am missing...

- I have been feeling...

- I am feeling guilty about...

- I miss the way they...

- I remember when we...

- I could use more...

- I can express these feelings creatively, like...

- I will be more compassionate to myself by...

- Who else is hurting, and what can I do to show them I am there for them?

- I want to emulate my (loved one's) (quality) by...

These are only a few ideas for prompts but searching online may give you more ideas to work with if you feel stuck. I sincerely hope this workbook helps you to further process your grief and your ability to move on in life.

CONCLUSION

This book has hopefully helped you to remember that you're not alone, that death is both unavoidable and an inevitable part of the human experience, and that grieving is a complicated, often messy task that is necessary for healing and moving forward with your life. You've read about the emotions and the financial considerations that both encompass and follow laying someone to rest, and you've learned that it's okay and necessary to love again and to rebuild your life in a way that puts you in the driver's seat. You've been educated on ways to try to connect with the deceased between this world and the next, and how to recharge the positive energy in your life to allow you to do this. You've explored breathwork and ways to cope with anxiety, depression, and a host of other mental health considerations that have come to light in your state of loss. You've learned how to help the young ones in your life who are also enduring the pain, and you've been cautioned about making life-changing decisions when perhaps you're not quite ready for that massive step. It's more than meditating or exercising, or even counseling, to process your pain; it's remembering that death is, indeed, a journey for everyone involved. It's realizing that just because a person no longer exists in this world, they are not gone. We are energy, and energy transforms, not dissipates.

I think in the end days, we have the greatest epiphanies about life when the ego falls away and our emotions are laid bare. We finally see clearly what life is all about. Life is about relationships and expressing how much we love those we've welcomed into our lives along the way. It's not about the cars, house, jobs, or money we make. Those things are nice, but they don't define who or what we are.

When you're in a calm state, it's important to discuss with those closest to you all the difficult things before you pass away. It's a comfort for those you leave behind to have your house, paperwork, and expenses sorted. It will ease the burden on them and allow your soul to find peace when it's time to meet your maker.

I hope that the stories shared by Elizabeth, Allison, and I help you to understand that you're not alone and that we're all in this together. Maybe we shouldn't look at death as the end, but as a beginning or the next plane of existence. I meditate, visualizing Amber, as healthy and beautiful, playing her guitar and doing all the things that she enjoyed and wanted to do in life but couldn't accomplish in the time she had on this earth. This makes me happy because I believe that she communicates with me from the other side to let me know that she's okay and that she finally receives the love she craves from a power greater than ourselves. You're loved, and you're not alone—not even for one second. I wish you all the love in the universe, my friends, and I pray that you seek those things that bring you peace in this life and the next.

129

Dear Reader, thank you for taking the time to read this book. I sincerely hope that you find peace and comfort and in some small way that this book did help! If you would be so kind to leave me a review on Amazon, I would appreciate it!

If you would like to read my own personal story of my journey with grief. I have another shorter book available on Amazon https://www.amazon.com/She-Was-Only-32-Connection-ebook/dp/B09X9GPQNW/

If you would like a free, printable, adult mandala coloring book with affirmations for dealing with grief please email me at southernroadspublishing@gmail.com

About the Author

Missy Richardson is a registered nurse, natural health practitioner, and author who loves adventure. Missy has been a nurse for over 30 years with a wealth of knowledge and experience. Raised in the Southern states, Missy has ventured to several territories in America as a travel nurse, in addition to global quests. Missy's encounters with diverse cultures and people resulted in the awareness of a common thread that connects humans at their core: love and loss. She was inspired to support others in mitigating their emotional challenges. This is her second book addressing the trauma and anguish, as well as the healing process of losing loved ones. The author shares her personal encounters, research, and methodologies to facilitate an opportunity to assist others in navigating through their unique journey.

References

Ashley Maselli Bio. (2022). www.betterhelp.com. https://www.betterhelp.com/advice/editorial_team/ashley-maselli/

Banks, R. (2020). How to deal with grief, loss, and death : a survivor's guide to coping with pain and trauma, and learning to live again. [Richard Banks]. https://www.everystep.org/filesimages/Grief%20and%20Loss/ATP%20Guide%20to%20Grief%20web.pdf

BetterHelp, E. T. (2022, August 26). 13 Best Relaxation Techniques For Anxiety | BetterHelp. www.betterhelp.com. https://www.betterhelp.com/advice/anxiety/13-best-relaxation-techniques-for-anxiety

Biteker, M., Duran, N. E., Civan, H. A., Gündüz, S., Gökdeniz, T., Kaya, H., & Özkan, M. (2009). Broken heart syndrome in a 17-year-old girl. European Journal of Pediatrics, 168(10), 1273–1275. https://doi.org/10.1007/s00431-008-0916-6

Blatner, A. (2005, February 19). Some Principles of Grief Work. https://www.blatner.com/adam/psyntbk/grief.htm

Canion, K. (2022, September 8). Give Yourself Permission To Love Again. #relationshipcoach. www.youtube.com; Coach Ken Canion. https://www.youtube.com/watch?v=DCDwv7najog

Chachar, A., Younus, S., & Ali, W. (2021, September). Developmental Understanding of Death and Grief Among Children During COVID-19 Pandemic: Application of Bronfenbrenner's Bioecological Model (S. Invitto, Ed.). www.frontiersin.org. https://www.frontiersin.org/articles/10.3389/fpsyt.2021.654584/full

Chaterjee, H. (2021, January 21). Websites To Read Books

For FREE Online! [UPDATED]. Bookwritten.com. https://bookwritten.com/where-to-read-books-for-free-online-websites/2489/

Christy Kessler. (2018, October 8). 5 Benefits of a Grief Journal. Funeral Basics. https://www.funeralbasics.org/benefits-grief-journal/

Comparison of [ebook] formats. (2022, August 23). Wikipedia. https://en.wikipedia.org/wiki/Comparison_of_e-book_formats

David Hawkins. (n.d.). Veritaspub.com; Veritas Publishers. Retrieved August 24, 2022, from https://veritaspub.com/dr-hawkins/

Dyregrov, A., & Dyregrov, K. (2008). Effective Grief and Bereavement Support: The Role of Family, Friends, Colleagues, Schools and Support Professionals. In Google Books (pp. 1–270). Jessica Kingsley Publishers. https://books.google.ca/books?hl=en&lr=&id=hSnU_sovDBEC&oi=fnd&pg=PP1&dq=supporting+ourselves+and+others+in+bereavement&ots=bkGa6aIjKK&sig=3T-DPxdhBnaLIQPHwgEsD-FlrO4#v=onepage&q=supporting%20ourselves%20and%20others%20in%20bereavement&f=false (Original work published 2022)

Ehmke, R. (2016, January 29). Helping Children Deal With Grief. Child Mind Institute; Child Mind Institute. https://childmind.org/article/helping-children-deal-grief/

8 best breathing techniques. (2020, July 27). www.medicalnewstoday.com. https://www.medicalnewstoday.com/articles/breathing-techniques#:~:text=The%20ALA%20recommend%20two%20different

Fadlon, I., Ramnath, S., Tong, P. K., & Camner McKay, L. (2020, May). Financial Life After the Death of a Spouse - Federal Reserve Bank of Chicago. www.chicagofed.org; Federal Reserve Bank of Chicago. https://www.chicagofed.org/publications/chicago-fed-letter/2020/438

Free Grief Workbook PDF - mind remake project. (2021, August 13). Mindremakeproject.org. https://mindremakeproject.org/2021/08/13/coping-with-loss-workbook/

Funeral Planning Checklist. (n.d.). Dignity Memorial. Retrieved August 25, 2022, from https://www.dignitymemorial.com/en-ca/plan-funeral-cremation/funeral-planning- checklist

Government of Canada, P. S. and P. C. (n.d.). Information archivée dans le Web. Publications.gc.ca. Retrieved September 17, 2022, from https://publications.gc.ca/collections/collection_2016/servcan/MP90-3-1-2-1997-eng.pdf

Greyson, B. (1983). The Near-Death Experience Scale Construction, Reliability, and Validity. The Journal of Nervous and Mental Disease, 171(6), 369–375. https://afanporsaber.com/wp-content/uploads/2014/01/The-near-death-experience-scale.-Construction-reliability-and-validity.pdf

Grief and Children. (2018, June). Aacap.org. https://www.aacap.org/AACAP/Families_and_Youth/Facts_for_Families/FFF-Guide/Children-And-Grief-008.aspx

Grief Reactions, Duration, and Tasks of Mourning - Whole Health Library. (n.d.). www.va.gov. Retrieved September 18, 2022, from https://www.va.gov/WHOLEHEALTHLIBRARY/tools/grief-reactions-duration-and-tasks-of-mourning.asp

Grief.com — – Podcasts. (n.d.). Grief.com. Retrieved September

13, 2022, from https://grief.com/podcasts/

Help Guide: Grief, Coping With Grief And Loss. (2019, January 7). HelpGuide.org. https://www.helpguide.org/articles/grief/coping-with-grief-and-loss.htm

Help Guide: Panic Attacks And Panic Disorders. (2019, May 7). HelpGuide.org. https://www.helpguide.org/articles/anxiety/panic-attacks-and-panic-disorders.htm

Hick, K. (2020, January 21). The Rollercoaster of Grief. www.centerforsharedinsight.com. https://www.centerforsharedinsight.com/blog/rollercoaster-grief/20065

How to deal with panic attacks. (2022, May 17). www.nhsinform.scot. https://www.nhsinform.scot/healthy-living/mental-wellbeing/anxiety-and-panic/how-to-deal-with-panic-attacks#:~:text=A%20panic%20attack%20is%20a

Hoy, T. (2022, July 11). The Amygdala: Function & Psychology Of Fight Or Flight (D. Brown, Ed.). www.betterhelp.com. https://www.betterhelp.com/advice/psychologists/the-amygdala-function-psychology-of-fight-or-flight/?utm_source=AdWords&utm_medium=Search_PPC_c&utm_term=PerformanceMax&utm_content=&network=x&placement=&target=&matchtype=&utm_campaign=17990185911&ad_type=responsive_pmax&adposition=&gclid=CjwK
CAjw6raYBhB7EiwABge5KpI_
hr8y8Ne6g_CLlsCL79S1dtz6eHh
mw5wNlyKf_85bGR07jYmT6RoCO5AQAvD_BwE

Hrvatin, V. (2021, June 24). Your brain on grief: Loss feels like a threat to survival. Healthing.ca. https://www.healthing.ca/wellness/mental-health/your-brain-on-grief-loss-feels-like-a-threat-to-survival

If You Are The Survivor | SSA. (n.d.). www.ssa.gov. Retrieved September 17, 2022, from https://www.ssa.gov/benefits/ survivors/ifyou.html#:~:text=Survivors%20Benefit%20 Amount

Irvin, J. (n.d.-a). 19 Ways to Raise Your Vibration. Sustainable Bliss | Self-Care and Meditation Membership. Retrieved August 25, 2022, from https://www.sustainableblissco.com/journal/ raising-your-vibration#:~:text=When%20something%20 vibrates%20at%20a

Irvin, J. (n.d.-b). Releasing Negative Energy with Tapping: EFT for Beginners. Sustainable Bliss | Self-Care and Meditation Membership. Retrieved September 5, 2022, from https:// www.sustainableblissco.com/journal/tapping

Irvin, J. (n.d.-a). 19 Ways to Raise Your Vibration. Sustainable Bliss | Self-Care and Meditation Membership. Retrieved August 25, 2022, from https://www.sustainableblissco.com/journal/ raising-your-vibration#:~:text=When%20something%20 vibrates%20at%20a

Irvin, J. (n.d.-b). Releasing Negative Energy with Tapping: EFT for Beginners. Sustainable Bliss | Self-Care and Meditation Membership. Retrieved September 5, 2022, from https:// www.sustainableblissco.com/journal/tapping

Is it Ok to be happy during grief? | Pathways. (n.d.). Pathways Home Health and Hospice. Retrieved September 17, 2022, from https://pathwayshealth.org/grief-support/is-it-ok-to-be-happy-during-grief/

J William Worden. (2018). Grief counseling and grief therapy

: a handbook for the mental health p ractitioner (5th ed.). Springer Publishing Company, LLC.

Jewell, C. (2021). Coping With Loss Workbook. Mind Remake Project.org.

Jones, K. W. (1985). Support For Grieving Kids. Home Healthcare Now, 3(4), 22–27. https://journals.lww.com/ homehealthcarenurseonline/Abstract/1985/07000/Support_ For_Grieving_Kids.6.aspx

Kadohisa, M. (2013). Effects of odor on emotion, with implications. Frontiers in Systems Neuroscience, 7. www.ncbi. nlm.nih.gov. https://doi.org/10.3389/fnsys.2013.00066

Kubala, J. (2018, June 12). Whole-Foods, Plant-Based Diet: A Detailed Beginner's Guide. Healthline. https://www.healthline.com/nutrition/plant-based-diet-guide#:~:text=Vegetables%3A%20Kale%2C%20 spinach%2C%20tomatoes

Lang, A., Fleiszer, A. R., Duhamel, F., Sword, W., Gilbert, K. R., & Corsini-Munt, S. (2011). Perinatal Loss and Parental Grief: The Challenge of Ambiguity and Disenfranchised Grief. OMEGA - Journal of Death and Dying, 63(2), 183–196. https:// doi.org/10.2190/om.63.2.e

Lawrence, D. (2022, July 12). The important financial steps to take after a spouse dies. The Globe and Mail. https://www. theglobeandmail.com/investing/globe-advisor/advisor-news/ article- financial-plan-death-spouse/

Lee, J. (2020, September 4). Grief worksheets: Simple PDFs for those experiencing a loss. Peacefully. https://guide.peacefully. com/resources/worksheets-to-help-those-coping-with-grief

Marty Slyter (Profile). (n.d.). www.linkedin.com. Retrieved August 24, 2022, from https://www.linkedin.com/in/marty-slyter-ba360232/

Maselli, A. (2022, August 23). Finding The Best Anxiety Podcast To Relieve Stress And Anxiety | BetterHelp. www.betterhelp.com. https://www.betterhelp.com/advice/anxiety/finding-the-best-anxiety-podcast-to-relieve-stress-and-anxiety/

McCoy, B. (2021, December 20). How your brain copes with grief, and why it takes time to heal. NPR. https://www.npr.org/sections/health-shots/2021/12/20/1056741090/grief-loss- holiday-brain-healing

McGinley, K. (n.d.). Karson McGinley. Chopra. Retrieved August 23, 2022, from https://chopra.com/bio/karson-mcginley#:~:text=Karson%20McGinley%20is%20the%20founder

McGinley, K. (2019, June 7). A Complete Guide to Raise Your Vibration. The Chopra Center. https://chopra.com/articles/a-complete-guide-to-raise-your-vibration

Medhus, E. (2015, November 8). I'm A Doctor. Here's Why I Think It's Possible To Communicate With The Dead. Mindbodygreen.com. https://www.mindbodygreen.com/0-22389/im-a-doctor-heres-why-i-think-its-possible-to-communicate-with-the-dead.html

Mediums Know How To Contact the Dead. (2016, April 15). www.thecircle.com. https://www.thecircle.com/uk/magazin/psychics/how-to-contact-the-dead.do

National Institute on Aging. (2017). Mourning the Death of a Spouse. National Institute on Aging. https://www.nia.nih.gov/

health/mourning-death-spouse

Oregonian/OregonLive, L. A. | T. (2018, October 23). 10 ways to communicate with the dead, according to an expert. Oregonlive. https://www.oregonlive.com/life-and-culture/ erry-2018/10/681847055948/10-ways-to-communicate-with-th.html

The Physics Classroom. (2019). Natural Frequency. Physicsclassroom.com. https://www.physicsclassroom.com/ class/sound/Lesson-4/Natural-Frequency

Pynoos, R. S. (2020). 56.3 TRAUMA-INFORMED SCREENING AND INTERVENTION FOR GRIEF AND CORE SYMPTOMS OF ADOLESCENTS WITH PTSD. Journal of the American Academy of Child & Adolescent Psychiatry, 59(10), S86. https://doi.org/10.1016/j.jaac.2020.07.356

Raypole, C. (2020, January 27). How to Help Someone Having a Panic Attack (A. Biggers, Ed.). Healthline. https://www. healthline.com/health/how-to-help-someone-having-a-panic-attack

rosegoldmama. (2021, February 11). Give Yourself Permission To Fall In Love With Yourself. The Savvy Working Mom. https://thesavvyworkingmom.com/give-yourself-permission-to-fall-in-love-with-yourself-2/

Saeed. (n.d.-a). Awaken | Satsang| Non Duality | Shaktipat | Spiritual Development & Meditation. Satsang with Saeed. Retrieved August 24, 2022, from https://www.nondualitylife. com/

Seeking Help and Support for Grief and Loss. (2014). Cancer. org; American Cancer Society. https://www.cancer.org/

treatment/end-of-life-care/grief-and-loss/depression-and-complicated-grief.html

Simeon, D. (2016, March 14). When Teens Lose Someone They Love. Your Teen Magazine. https://yourteenmag.com/health/teenager-mental-health/help-a-grieving-teenager

Slyter, M. (2012). Creative Counseling Interventions for Grieving Adolescents. Journal of Creativity in Mental Health, 7(1), 17–34. ERIC. https://doi.org/10.1080/15401383.2012.65 7593

Smith, S. (2018, April 10). 5-4-3-2-1 coping technique for anxiety. www.urmc.rochester.edu. https://www.urmc.rochester.edu/behavioral-health-partners/bhp-blog/april-2018/5-4-3-2-1-coping-technique-for-anxiety.aspx

Szuhany, K. L., Malgaroli, M., Miron, C. D., & Simon, N. M. (2021). Prolonged Grief Disorder: Course, Diagnosis, Assessment, and Treatment. FOCUS: The Journal of Lifelong Learning in Psychiatry, 19(2), 161–172. Psychiatry Online. https://doi.org/10.1176/appi.focus.20200052

Wallace, T. (n.d.). Types of Grief: Grief Reactions, Grief Symptoms, and FAQs for Your Own Grief Experience | Eterneva. www.eterneva.com. Retrieved September 10, 2022, from https://www.eterneva.com/resources/types-of-grief

Wendy Ann Zellea. (n.d.). www.amazon.com. Retrieved September 12, 2022, from https://www.amazon.com/Wendy-Ann-Zellea/e/B004KN41QW%3Fref=dbs_a_mng_rwt_scns_share

Williamson, J. (2018, April 11). 21 Grief Journaling Prompts to Get the Healing Energy Flowing. Healing Brave. https://

healingbrave.com/blogs/all/grief-journaling-prompts

Zellea, W. A. (2020, December 30). Death is Not the End of Our Life Force Energy. Gaia. https://www.gaia.com/article/death-not-end-our-life-force-energy

141

mourning-ribbon-with-frame-concept, blue-powder-pastel-with-hand-drawn-flowers-background, watercolor-green-leaves-wreath-with-gold-circle, hand-drawn-condolence-card-template : Freepik.com".
This cover has been designed using assets from Freepik.com

www.ingramcontent.com/pod-product-compliance
Lightning Source LLC
LaVergne TN
LVHW041224080426
835508LV00011B/1066

*9 7 9 8 9 8 7 2 9 8 5 4 1 *